D1625387

Decision Making for First-Time Managers

Decision Making for First-Time Managers

W. H. Weiss

amacom

American Management Association

This book is available at a special discount when ordered in bulk quantities. For information, contact Special Sales Department, AMACOM, a division of American Management Association, 135 West 50th Street, New York, NY 10020

Library of Congress Cataloging in Publication Data

Weiss, W. H., 1918-
   Decision making for first-time managers.

   Includes index.
   1. Decision-making. I. Title.
HD30.23.W45   1985   658.4′03   84-45794
ISBN 0-8144-5809-2

Printing number

10 9 8 7 6 5 4 3 2 1

*To my wife, Ernestine, for
her patience and understanding
regarding my need to write.*

Contents

Chapter One   **Making Decisions:**
A Supervisory Responsibility   1

Understanding Decision Making / Level of Decision Making / Routine Decisions / Being Technically Aware / Decision-Making Strategy / The Art of Decision Making / Dealing with Uncertainty / Responsible Decision Making / The Stress of Decision Making / Self-Confidence / Confidence in Making Decisions / Technique and Procedure / Developing Skill at Making Decisions

Chapter Two   **Problem Solving**
and Decision Making   20

Basic Understanding of the Problem / Guidelines for Problem Solving / Staying on Top of Problems / Solving a Problem Through Change / Effectiveness in Handling Change / The Pitfalls of Problem Solving / Insight as a Factor in Making Decisions / Decisiveness / Delegating Responsibility and Decisions / When a Decision Should Not Be Made / Group Decision Making / Strategy for Problem Solving

Chapter Three   **Factors that Influence**
                                  Decisions   42

The Risk / Contending with Risks / Positive
Thinking / Human Factors / Personal Factors /
Pressure and Stress / Costs / Policy / Change /
Why People Resist Change / Promoting Accept-
ance / Making Decisions Involving Change /
Power and Authority

Chapter Four   Deterrents and Hindrances—
                    Aids and Simplifications   74

Procrastination / Unspecifiable Risk Procrasti-
nation / Fear of Making the Decision / Fear of a
Rub / Worry that a Decision Might Be Regretted
/ Stimulants of Worry / Rationalization / Con-
flict / Loyalty / Commitment / Social and Per-
sonal Constraints / Degree of Commitment and
Entrapment / Commitment Warnings / Getting
Facts / When to Stop Seeking Facts / Bias and
Prejudice / Bias About Safety Issues / Heuristic
Reasoning / Intuition and Hunch / Common
Sense / Sound Decisions / Credibility / Experi-
ence / The Problem of Time / The Value of Quick
Thinking / Developing Quick Thinking / Snap
Decisions / Planning Helps Decision Making /
Speed in Making Decisions / Tricks to Avoid
Making Decisions

Chapter Five   Communication:
                    Key to Making Decisions   120

Communicating Information / Verifying That
You're Understood / Informal Communications
/ Bypassing / Participation / The Benefits of

Participation / The Problems with Participative Decision Making / Meetings / Explaining Your Decisions

Chapter Six   **Analysis Procedures**   **134**

Mathematical Techniques and Tools / Quantifiable Factors / Unquantifiable Factors / Decision-Making Tools / Statistical Analysis / Marginal and Cost-Benefit Analysis / Operations Research / Risk Analysis and Risk Preference / The Computer's Influence

Chapter Seven   **Making a Choice**   **151**

Premises / Considering Alternatives / The Problems of Evaluation / Selecting Alternatives / Policy as an Aid / The Decision Tree / Evaluating a Decision's Importance / The Best Decisions

Chapter Eight   **Implementing the Decision and Following Up**   **164**

Taking Action / Acting Without Deciding / Testing a Decision / Following Up / Feedback / Controlling the Effects of a Decision / Reviewing Your Decision / When Your Decision Is Not Accepted / When Decisions Go Bad / Resolving a Bad Decision / A Perspective on Decision Making

Index   **176**

Chapter One

Making Decisions: A Supervisory Responsibility

Many people in supervisory positions today are unsure of themselves when making decisions. Although they know that making decisions is probably the most important part of the job, most new first-line managers* have little if any experience in this function of management. It is therefore understandable that they do not know how to go about making sound decisions, especially when those decisions involve people.

When it comes to making decisions, no supervisory position is an easy one. Many skills are required, including being technically aware, knowing how to deal with uncertainty, and having confidence in one's ability to handle all types of problems. In addition, to be effective, managers must understand the strategy, tech-

---

*Some people would preserve a distinction between the terms *manager* and *supervisor*. Yet in recent years the distinction has become less and less apparent. The precise term used often depends more on a particular company's preference than on substantive differences in the responsibilities of those called managers and those called supervisors. Thus, the terms *manager* and *supervisor* will be used interchangeably throughout this book. *Manager*, however, will be understood to refer to individuals holding *first-line* supervisory positions, unless specified otherwise.

nique, and procedure involved in making decisions and be able to apply them on the job.

Understanding Decision Making

The ability to make sensible decisions calmly and with reasonable speed is helpful in any position in life. It is especially so for supervisors because they are so closely involved with people. One sure way to differentiate between a better-than-average supervisor and a mediocre one is to judge them on their decision-making ability. Those who are decisive and effective gain the respect of both their subordinates and their superiors.

Many first-line managers, however, feel uneasy with this responsibility. Yet even high-level executives hesitate and are not always confident when faced with making an important decision. Understanding the whys and hows of decision making is an asset to people because the knowledge tends to lessen the tension and pressure they feel when they are required to reason, analyze, and act on a problem. By learning the process of how decisions are made and by recognizing the factors involved, people improve their managerial ability.

Initially, supervisors may look to their own qualifications and the training they've received to perfect their decision-making skill. How their knowledge is influenced by the many external factors that affect decisions then needs to be resolved. Although a manager's orders or instructions invariably bring action, they are just the culmination of a procedure that may have involved consideration of people, conditions, and the circumstances of the particular situation.

The experienced supervisor has an advantage over the neophyte when a decision must be made. This is not to say, however, that experience is a prime requisite for effective decision making, since then only the older, been-around-a-long-time person could be expected to make good ones. Experience is a valuable aid primarily when snap decisions must be made. The experienced person remembers similar problems and situations and draws upon this memory to solve the current problem. The value of experience should not be taken lightly. High-level executives attain their positions through a series of upward managerial steps,

2

with each higher position demanding more skill and ability in making decisions and requiring that they call more and more on their training and experience.

Level of Decision Making

One of the basic principles of good management is that decisions should be made at the lowest feasible level in the organization. This puts decisions as close as possible to the area where they are to be implemented. With this precept, any attempts to avoid making decisions where they should be made or to pass them to a higher authority must be resisted. Thus, a decision that rightfully falls within the responsibility of a supervisor should be made by the supervisor. Under such a style of managing, people not only have responsibility, they are also able to show their authority.

A first-line manager can be criticized for trying to avoid making a decision only if the manager knows that he or she is responsible for making it. Passing the buck occurs most frequently in organizations where responsibilities have not been clearly defined. Higher-level managers must refrain from taking over responsibilities that they have delegated to their supervisors. Although such managers unquestionably have the right to make lower-level decisions, they should not arbitrarily do so without good justification. When planning is a major function in an organization and the responsibilities of individuals are clearly defined, the responsibility for making decisions should never be usurped. If supervisors are not permitted to make important decisions, ones that they know they are qualified to make, they will soon feel that *any* decision they make is important. The practice, sooner or later, will affect priorities and assumed responsibilities. The result can only be inefficiency and a loss of effectiveness on the part of the supervisors.

Routine Decisions

To cover all the facets of the art of decision making, a distinction should be made between routine decisions and true decisions. By far the larger number of decisions made by supervisors are recognized by them and others as routine—they hardly justify being called decisions. Some supervisors feel that up to 95 percent of all the decisions they make can be labeled as routine. Thus, they are of the opinion that decision making is overplayed as a major managerial responsibility. Since for long periods of time supervisors may "decide" only problems whose solutions are to them self-evident, it is logical that they would feel this way.

The procedure for making decisions presented in this book is intended to require some thought and study by the first-line manager. Decisions that result from following the procedure may not be easily identified, since most people tend to respond automatically, even in very complicated situations. A true decision is required so infrequently that supervisors may resist making it until a deadline approaches or the situation changes. In support of this stand is the axiom that it is best to put off a true decision until it must be made. A frequent comment heard in this regard is "I'll sleep on it before I decide." While this may smack somewhat of showmanship—giving the impression of deliberation and reflection—it also lends credence to the belief that the mind often works best without conscious control.

Being Technically Aware

When you are called upon to make a decision that is innovative or that will result in a basic change in an existing procedure, you must be fully informed about the technical details of the undertaking. New and original ideas are developed and promulgated best by informed and knowledgeable individuals, ones who have a good understanding of the basics and have studied the subject extensively.

For example, if you are required to make a decision about buying a word processor or a computer, you must be familiar with the capabilities and features of various systems available to you. Otherwise, you could not make a sound decision on which system would be best for your organization. Similarly, if you are faced with a decision concerning a work procedure, you should be aware of the present procedure in its entirety, including the principles that govern it. Having such knowledge, you could decide what effect a change would have. To make a sound decision relating to the behavior of people, you will stand a better chance if you know them individually, how they think and why they behave as they do. Being cognizant of such matters will enable you to properly and effectively employ the stimuli that will cause them to perform more efficiently.

Decision-Making Strategy

Everyone on the job makes decisions that are related to his or her position and the environment. Supervisors and higher-level managers have the added responsibility for decisions that affect others. The environment of the decision maker and the position he or she assumes affect the decision-making process, but basically, a decision maker selects a course of action from available alternatives in order to achieve a desired result.

First, a choice must be made; if there is only one way to go, no decision is necessary. Second, making decisions requires use of mental faculties at the conscious level; logic is essential, yet emotion will also play a part. Third, a purpose is behind each decision; the decision is made to achieve or reach some objective.

The process of making a decision evolves in five phases in the mind of an individual—for instance, a first-line manager:

1. The manager understands the situation and is aware of the factors that should be considered. His or her education and experience may tend to complicate matters, in that the factors may appear innumerable.
2. The manager recognizes the true problem. This is so important that when a person is sure that the problem is correctly defined, it is already partially solved.
3. The search for and analysis of available alternatives begins. Logic plays a part in working out the consequences of various alternatives.
4. The manager selects the best alternative. It may be only slightly better than a number of other options.
5. The decision is accepted by the organization. The person or persons responsible for implementing it do so.

These five phases form the strategy of the decision-making process. The techniques vary, depending on the type of decision to be made. Two types are most common: the initiation type and the approval type. In the initiation type, the decision maker originates the process; in the approval type, the decision maker receives recommendations and approves their implementation. The attributes needed by supervisors in initiating decisions differ from those needed in approving recommendations, in that with approval decisions, group interactions play a big part. A supervisor who is people-oriented, who recognizes the capabilities of others and can call upon them for help, will probably handle the initiation type of decisions very well. A supervisor who is decisive and dependable can be expected to do well with approval-type decisions.

The Art of Decision Making

Supervising and making decisions go together. All supervisors must make decisions, and many decisions must be made when conditions are uncertain. Thus, supervisors must be able to handle uncertainty if they are to carry out their responsibilities. Although most supervisors feel inadequate when they are uncertain, making decisions is one of the important functions of managing. Moreover, they must have the courage to make decisions without fretting over them and expecting to have a perfect answer for every problem that arises. Alert managers know that they must decide trivial matters quickly and spend most of their time on major and serious problems. Management expects supervisors to get things done through people, not by themselves. Decision making distinguishes managers from nonmanagers in the organization.

Supervisors make decisions about equipment operation and production rates. They decide what jobs are to be done and what tools are to be used. They make schedules, and they decide to whom to assign the work. Supervisors are decision makers, whether they supervise 2 or 20 people.

The productivity of the workforce depends on the decisions made by first-line managers. Some of their decisions are good, and some undoubtedly are bad. No supervisor always makes the right decision. But the greater the number of good decisions, the more productive the workforce is going to be. It follows that supervisors can improve their overall performance by becoming better decision makers.

Are there formulas to be followed to assure the making of good decisions? Generally, the higher a person's position in management, the more likely it is that he or she follows a procedure or method of analysis in making major decisions. In addition, as the person makes decisions and sees the results, training takes place and experience is gained. Yet no supervisor aspiring to a better position in an organization should be content with this. Universities offer business and management courses to invididuals rising through the management levels in their organizations. Those individuals dedicated to their work and wanting to advance take advantage of such courses.

As for who will make good decisions, look to the enthusiastic person, the one who shows innovation and imagination when expressing himself or herself. Such an individual demonstrates both creativity and versatility. He or she is not satisfied to handle today's problems the same as yesterday's. Decision making involves treading a path between two extremes—procrastination or impulsive action. Yet when a call for action is urgent, even a poor decision may be better than none. Since making a clear, decisive judgment is sometimes difficult, managerial decisions often turn out to be compromises, even though such solutions are appalling to the strong, committed-to-the-job executive.

Dealing with Uncertainty

Uncertainty, as noted, is part of the game of making decisions. Supervisors who know how to contend with it make decisions that take it into account. Supervisors who are unable to deal with it have problems. Either they will make poor decisions or they will postpone them to wait for the uncertainty to be resolved. Still, uncertainty in decision making can be dealt with. Adopting a prescribed course of action will result in far more good decisions than bad ones. Remember, you need not be right all the time, only most of the time.

In order to deal with uncertainty, managers must recognize

the problem. There is no uncertainty about the various courses of action available to them. Such alternatives either exist or they don't. The uncertainty lies with the consequences of the courses. Making decisions is difficult because there can be several consequences to each alternative. For example, when a supervisor hands out a work assignment, the worker receiving it could: (1) do a good job, (2) do a poor job, or (3) not do the job at all. To make matters worse, whether the assignment brings about a favorable or unfavorable result sometimes depends on other factors beyond the knowledge or control of the supervisor. The worker could be ill, tired, in a bad frame of mind, or not paying attention. These factors, uncontrollable at the moment, are responsible for the uncertainty surrounding the supervisor's decision. If the supervisor knew that the worker was well, rested, in a receptive mood, and paying attention, the results of the decision to make the assignment would be more certain. Even then, a manager can never be absolutely certain, because people change their minds, giving misleading impressions, and are often simply unpredictable. Nevertheless, the supervisor must deal with this uncertainty in some manner. Mathematicians and statisticians have developed various techniques for dealing with uncertainty. Although many of these are impractical or not applicable to the decisions facing supervisors, some are simple and relatively easy to use. The subject is discussed in a later chapter of this book.

When faced with making a decision when they are uncertain, insecure first-line managers will attempt to dodge the issue or try to share the responsibility with other people. They may solicit the advice of others, including their superiors, when they unquestionably should make the decision themselves. Secure supervisors recognize that they cannot sidestep taking some risks; they simply use their best judgment and hope for the best.

Even the most capable supervisors are not infallible. Like the average person, they are occasionally guilty of mistakes, including errors in judgment. Everyone has a bad day now and then despite all efforts to avoid it. Although infallibility cannot be assured in making decisions, there are certain steps that can be taken to minimize the possibility of making bad decisions. Good decision makers take their time. They consult with knowledgeable persons, and they are very thorough in searching through the records for historical information. In addition, they may laboriously list the advantages and disadvantages of all the alternatives. So when they finally make their decisions, they know in their own minds that they have done their best.

Responsible Decision Making

One of the most difficult lessons for a first-line manager to learn is that making decisions demands toughness and tenacity. It's possible to become so emotionally involved with one of your people that you can't make the decision you should make concerning him or her. You eventually learn that every problem and every personality calls for a specific approach. When you alone are affected by the outcome of a decision you make, you have more leeway because you're answerable only to yourself. Decisions you make on the job deserve more of your consideration, since they affect other people and the company you work for. You tread dangerous ground when you make decisions unsupported by logic or reasoning. Better that you gain the trust and respect of your people by knowing exactly what you're doing and why you're doing it.

As you learn to carry out all the responsibilities of a supervisor, you become aware of the steps you must follow in order to make good decisions. You see that when you have a problem, you must first define it. Then you must get facts and data relative to it, search for alternative answers, consider the probable outcome of each alternative, and finally select the best one.

You can use this analytical technique with just about every decision you make. If you feel that many of your decisions are too minor to justify going through the steps, you should do it anyway to get into the habit. The more frequently you do, the more effective you'll become in making decisions. To carry the process further, you might want to make a record of how you reached certain decisions. Then, when you learn how your decision fared, you can refer to your notes to determine why the decision proved to be sound or unsound.

When you must make a quick decision, you can do nothing more than call upon whatever knowledge and information you have at the moment. But it would be foolhardy to follow this procedure with decisions where you have more time. Making snap decisions when you don't have to causes resentment and a loss of respect. One of the basic rules for responsible decision making is to allow time and patience to prevail. Listen to and consider the suggestions people offer you. It's smart to assume that you don't have all the pertinent information. Why not consult with other individuals who may be able to contribute something critical?

The first-line manager is the key to giving workers increased responsibility. How much power do you pass on to your people to make decisions about their work? Do you insist that they check with you on every questionable matter, or do you tell them to use their best judgment? How do you react when they make a poor decision? Your answers to these questions can make a big difference in terms of the amount of responsibility your people believe they have been given for their work. If a decision made by one of your people works out well, you should talk about it to others as well as personally commend the employee involved. This is the way to encourage people to be more responsible and conscientious.

When a supervisor makes a decision that should logically be made by someone who works for him or her, the supervisor is denying that person the experience of studying a problem, reaching a conclusion, and taking action. Remember that everyone gets satisfaction from an accomplishment and feels good about it, especially if that accomplishment is important work and contributes to the department's objectives.

The Stress of Decision Making

Making decisions is stressful to people who are very much aware of the risk of suffering serious losses from whatever course of action they take. Additional stress is experienced if they worry about the difficulty of reversing their decisions should that be necessary. With these uncertainties to worry about, it is understandable why decision makers are reluctant to make irrevocable choices.

The most common expressions of stress are revealed in feeling uncertain, being inclined to hesitate, and tending to vacillate. Many executives in business and industry report sleepless nights, loss of interest in eating, and almost unbearable tensions. Other symptoms of stress that are experienced at the time of making a difficult decision include feelings of apprehensiveness, a wish to escape having to make a choice, and self-blame for having allowed oneself to get into a situation where all available alternatives seem unsatisfactory. While first-line managers' decisions seldom affect the destiny and future of the company as seriously as the decisions of the company's top executives, supervisors may feel the stress of their decisions just as much. The intensity of stress seems to depend on how great the possible loss might be if the decision maker were to select a poor alternative. You will feel more stress if your decision could cost your company $50,000 than if it could cost $5,000.

At one time or another, all decision makers are likely to face situations that cause extreme stress. However, with day-to-day decisions where risks are minimal and losses would be inconsequential, correspondingly less stress is felt. Yet even these decisions may have an effect on the quality of fact-finding and evaluation that decision makers employ. If a decision seems trivial, you may not spend much time thinking about it before acting. But when you must make a decision that will affect your future welfare, you may find it painful to commit yourself, particularly when you know there are some risks and costs no matter which course of action you follow. The obvious way to cope with this situation is, of course, to avoid making the decision. We all are inclined to procrastinate to some degree whether or not we are aware of it. Furthermore, if we refuse to be guilty of procrastinating, we can substitute a rationalization for ignoring a worrying doubt. There is no question that procrastinating and rationalizing are means of avoiding decision making and a way of coping with its stress. In reality, though, they can be just as detrimental to making good decisions as acting impulsively.

Decision makers who have a high batting average are careful to avoid making decisions when they are under stress. They've learned from experience that it's better to delay a decision than to make it when they're angry or upset. Decisions made with emotion as a basis are never as good as those made through reasoning and logical thinking. But most decisions made in business and industry are based on much more than just logic and reason. All of us are influenced by emotion. It plays a large part in our lives.

We must learn to handle it if we are to get along well with people and have a successful career.

People who have a decision to make think and act in two ways. They either reason the problem out, or they decide what to do through emotion. While reasoning involves dealing with logic and facts, emotion concerns one's feelings. Most people consider themselves experts on logic and reason. They honestly believe that the statements they make and the acts they perform are logically and reasonably thought out beforehand. Yet studies have shown that 20 percent of their decisions are based on reason and 80 percent on emotion!

Making decisions under stress is not easy. Sometimes your decision may be clearly right but difficult to carry out. Other times, you may need exceptional wisdom or inspiration to come up with the best thing to do. Whatever problem you face, be sure you take time to focus on *what* needs to be decided and what the objectives are. If you have an interpersonal decision to make, you must plan when and where you will discuss the problem with the person involved. If the person is emotional when the subject is brought up, allow some time for cooling off before you again get together. Choose a time when neither of you will feel stress or tension and the atmosphere is relaxed. You will find yourself better able to reason out a decision that is satisfactory to both of you.

Self-Confidence

Lack of self-confidence is a major stumbling block all first-line managers must contend with if they are to realize their fullest potential as decision makers. Unless overcome, this obstacle may limit them to only partial success in carrying out the responsibilities of their jobs. But they should have no cause for despair regarding this. Self-confidence can be developed with practice and experience. Although it takes time and effort, once self-confidence has been established, it is seldom lost.

Since self-confidence means so much to people in responsible positions, let's examine self-confidence and determine what it consists of and how you can recognize it in yourself. When you are confident, you feel that you can meet any demand made upon you.

A self-confident person acts as if success were the only possible outcome of any task or project he or she takes on. Such a person doesn't waste any effort worrying about problems that may never arise. Furthermore, such a person applies his or her efforts only to situations that require change.

Guilt feelings are a deterrent to self-confidence. Often a person who feels guilty about something he or she has said or done may refuse to admit that any wrong was committed. The person may also try to put the matter out of his or her mind. But when a mistake has been made, it would be better for the person to admit it and get on with other matters.

While success may bolster self-confidence, failure may tear it down. Depending on people's attitudes, failures can make them fearful to try again, or failures can give them the courage and strength to continue to take on new responsibilities and to make tough decisions. The best viewpoint is to expect to be a good decision maker and then work diligently at it to assure that you are. As for failing to always make good decisions, keep in mind that people who have been successful in everything they've tried have set their goals too low. They could probably hold jobs with more responsibility if they were willing to take the risk of going after them.

Nothing can destroy self-confidence more than being overly sensitive to what others think of you. Don't look for approval as a guide for what to say and do. Decide and act on the basis of what you think is right and fair and you will lead rather than follow. Be yourself and you'll have more admirers than if you were primarily concerned with pleasing others. Just as important, developing the sense of knowing what is right and wrong will increase your confidence in yourself.

Confidence in Making Decisions

Competent managers do not like to have decisions made for them. They feel that they would be abdicating their responsibilities if they permitted this to happen. You should not entrust important decisions to other. To pass them off is to give up your personal obligations—literally, how you are going to live your life. Avoiding decisions that are rightfully yours in reality puts you out of the game. Making your own decisions shows maturity and personal responsibility.

Some people believe that many decisions will be made for them if they just wait long enough. Other people believe that many decisions are unnecessary because "what is going to happen, will happen." In some situations, decisions cannot be postponed. Letting time and the natural course of events make your decisions for you means that you are resigned to accept whatever happens, that you'll get by somehow if the worst happens. The truth of the matter is that people are better off and happier when they have more control over their destiny.

You may decide something simply in order to get rid of a problem, thereby getting out from under a situation that bothers you. Although you may succeed at the time with this approach, you will often be sorry later. Such decisions are usually made without a lot of thought and consideration; thus, there's a strong likelihood that you will make more bad decisions than good ones.

If you feel that looking at both the pros and cons of a situation on which you must act is usually a waste of time, you are probably impulsive. You'd be better off it you got in the habit of considering the advantages and disadvantages of all the alternatives. Although weighing consequences takes time, by doing it you get a broader perspective of the art of making decisions. To be able to see a problem from several viewpoints is an aid to the decision-making process because this makes you flexible. Being flexible enables you to change your mind and come up with a better decision.

Checking decisions to see how they worked out is commendable because it indicates not only that you are curious about the outcome of a decision for its own sake but also that you want to discover the outcome in order to make better decisions in the future.

Your confidence that you will make a good decision may suffer if you feel confused when you have to make an important one. Your confusion may be caused by asking the wrong questions or asking too many questions. But you may also be confused because you don't have a good way to arrive at a decision. Whatever, you give up hope and guess. Perhaps you are not confused, but headstrong instead. Then you may confuse opinion with fact and feel that your decisions are always right; you don't want to be bothered with facts because you have already made up your mind. Even if you aren't confused, you may frequently oversimplify a problem and are then just as likely to make a bad decision as a person who is confused.

Do you lack confidence when making decisions because you have second thoughts about whether they are right? You shouldn't let this bother you. Most decision makers are unsure of themselves a good bit of the time. They wonder whether they considered all the facts, overlooked something, or used faulty reasoning. People normally ask themselves such questions. If they review and analyze their decisions, they learn how to improve them. However, if they subject themselves to useless post-mortem questioning, they may easily lose their self-confidence and even succumb to deceiving themselves in trying to justify their decisions.

It's tough to have to admit you made a poor decision. It's also a blow to your self-confidence. Yet if you stick with your decision after you realize that it is wrong, all you do is make matters worse. Very few decisions should be thought of as absolute. Decisions are only as good as the facts and information they were based on. Any decision could prove to be bad, regardless of who made it. Decision makers must be prepared to change their decisions should that become necessary.

If you feel that your decisions are usually poor no matter how hard you try, your self-confidence will certainly be affected adversely. In all likelihood, you make decisions in a reckless manner. To compound the problem, your bad decisons are probably remembered, thus refueling your defeatist attitude. You may eventually reach the point where you will take no responsibility for any decision you make.

To make no decision is usually preferable to making a bad decision. Taking action does not guarantee that a problem is handled or that benefits will be realized. You should be aware that no decision is the best course to follow with some problems, especially when you know that you lack information.

Your self-confidence that you can make good decisions is strong if you believe that consulting with others about those decisions can only confuse the issue. Yet such thinking is probably based on whose help you have been seeking. Many people are ready to give you advice, but not all are qualified to assist you with your particular problem. The right people, those who can help you make a better decision, are those who have previously made decisions on matter similar to yours. Of course, if you have already made up your mind about a problem, talking to other people may be disconcerting because a new slant or more information might come out of your discussions. Be aware, too, that if you have higher status than the people you consult, they may not be of much help simply because they may be afraid to speak up or disagree with you.

How do you feel about helping other people with their decisions? If you feel competent at this, it says much for your self-confidence. Yet you may want to consider what this means. People who feel confident in making decisions for others are not necessarily confident in making decisions for themselves. Then again, just the opposite may also be true. Whatever, if your advice is asked for, take a good look at yourself. You probably are a better decision maker than you think.

Technique and Procedure

Every first-line manager early in his or her career learns that the job entails continuously making decisions. Although making a decision isn't a new experience, differences in the type of decisions to be made are apparent, and the consequences of those decisions have become important. A good supervisor soon realizes that he or she should formulate a procedure for making decisions that will assure that all alternatives are considered and that each decision made is the best one possible under the circumstances. In doing this, the supervisor should keep in mind that:

1. There is no one best way to make all decisions.
2. The steps of making a decision invariably overlap.
3. Conscious as well as unconscious factors influence many decisions.
4. Decisions made on the basis of logic alone may be faulty.

A supervisor doesn't have to be on the job very long before he or she realizes that making decisions in not a separate responsibility of the job but is included in nearly everything he or she says or does; also, that decision making is so akin to problem solving that supervisors are faced with more problem decisions than opportunity decisions.

Usually, first-line managers who make good decisions are soon promoted to better jobs. However, many managers are novices in learning the best procedure to follow to perfect their decision-making skill. Although there is no surefire way to be a success, here are some guidelines to get you started on the right path:

1. Concentrate on the objective of a decision you must make. Know what you want to achieve. Hold off making any decision until you are sure you know all that is involved.

2. Constantly reconsider the objective and be ready to change your approach if you sense that you should. Be flexible to the extent that you can readily adjust to new information. Changing circumstances may require you to make a new decision. To reverse or modify a decision does not mean you're inept as a decision maker.

3. Accept the advice and recommendations of others but rely on your own judgment and experience when it comes to making the decision. Don't automatically follow an expert's advice.

4. Give your hunch or intuition considerable weight. Hunches emanate from more than just facts and information; they should be considered along with the other bases of your decisions.

5. Be fearless and aggressive when making a decision. Meekness does not convey assuredness. Major changes can be made more easily than minor ones. But be sure your attack has been planned and well thought out.

6. See that your decision fits the particular circumstances and that you're not making it because such a decision worked before. It is risky to assume that two situations are identical and can therefore be handled the same way. Priorities, directions, and people change. You must judge each situation as separate and distinct from all others.

7. Consider the preferences of other people, including your boss and his or her boss. It is sheer folly to make a decision that conflicts with their thinking unless you have a very convincing argument to back it up.

8. Take your time, especially with important decisions. The more impact the decisions will have, the more time you should devote to them.

9. Be wary of selecting your first choice of alternatives. Experienced decision makers say that you can almost always find a better one. Consider as many alternatives as possible.

10. Be prepared to change course once you act. Decisions often trigger new problems, and the reactions to a decision can alter a situation greatly.

Developing Skill at Making Decisions

When you make the right decision, no one notices. When you make the wrong one, everyone does. Knowing how to deal professionally with people relationships and make more competent decisions will help you to become a more effective supervisor. Supervisors usually need all the help they can get.

You might think that the more decisions you make, the more skilled you'd become at it. But decision making is not like making a speech or driving a car. The number of decisions you make has nothing to do with your skill at making them or how they turn out. The art of decision making does not receive a lot of attention from educators and personnel training groups. We take lessons to learn how to drive or to become good at golf, but rely on our own instincts to learn how to make decisions. If it is believed that making decisions is easy, that is simply not true.

In order to make good decisions, you have to understand values and be able to weigh one thing against another. If a decision or series of decisions is to help you reach your goal, you must first decide what your goal is—that becomes your basic decision. For most people, it's a difficult one because they work at a job and go through life without having any clear objectives.

How do your learn to make good decisions? Some people say that you can learn only from experience. If you pursued the subject further and asked how you could get experience, these people would say that making bad decisions will provide you the experience. But that's not the total answer. To learn to make good decisions, you must possess knowledge about the problems you face and develop your analytical skills. You also need to acquire confidence in your abilities. Last but not least, you must be willing to take risks.

Managers are paid to make decisions, many of which involve risks. Invariably, you will make some poor decisions, but that is how you learn. When you learn how to deal with a bad decision, you will have less fear of the consequences of making a mistake. If you make a bad decision, you should review how you reached it and determine where you went wrong. Now you're ready to modify your decision or make a new one.

Another facet of decision making that deserves consideration is the motivation behind making one. Some people are directed mainly by their minds, others mainly by their emotions. The decisions that derive from the mind are the conscious and logical ones; those from the emotions are the subconscious and intuitive ones. Even the most logical people make some decisions emotionally, and the most emotional make some logically. Which are the better decisions, the ones that arise from feelings or the ones that arise from reason?

The great majority of decisions affect people. Since people by their very nature feel as well as think, a logical decision may fail if those on whom its success depends reject it for emotional reasons. A decision you make about yourself, no matter how logical, may not be right if it doesn't feel right. The most lasting and sound decisions contain both reason and emotion. It is the balance or proportion that is crucial to whether or not a particular decision is good or bad.

When making a decision concerning someone, you have a much better chance of winning the person's acceptance and support if you consider his or her feelings. A major reason for much of the discontent in business and industry today stems from the exclusion of people from participation in the decisions that affect them. If management asked employees to become involved in these decisions, many demonstrations, sit-downs, and strikes might be prevented.

In developing your skill at decision making, vary your style to fit the situation. No single style works in all cases. Make some decisions by consulting with your subordinates, peers, and superiors. Make other decisions alone. When you talk to people about a problem, ask only for information sometimes and ask for their recommendations at other times.

Being sure you understand the problem is the most difficult step in making a decision. It is the most important step as well. It is important for a supervisor to make good decisions. But in order to make a good decision, it is first necessary to correctly identify the problem at hand.

Chapter Two

Problem Solving and Decision Making

You can view your problems on the job in several ways, but basically you have a problem when something stands in the way of reaching your objective. You also have a problem when what you expect to happen doesn't happen. For instance, as a production supervisor, many things can prevent you from reaching your daily or monthly quota. A shortage of raw material, labor, or equipment can become a problem if you haven't planned for it.

Problem solving and decision making are supervisory functions that go together. In fact, problem solving can be said to be decision making. Anything that you do in planning, organizing, scheduling, directing, and controlling that requires you to choose a course of action from among several alternatives is decision making. Managers must continually decide whether to do something or not do it, to say something or remain silent, to correct something or let it continue as it is. They should be aware, however, that even if they do none of these things, they are nevertheless making a choice—it is a decision not to make a change.

Problems are best solved through a systematic procedure, although you may not be conscious that you are following it with minor or routine matters. Yet decision making need not always be systematic. Sometimes you make a decision based on your intuition or hunch. When you are pressed for time, a snap judgment may be your only recourse.

Basic Understanding of the Problem

A supervisor's decision can be no better than the information it's based upon. If you can't ask people to look up relevant information about a problem you face, you can gather all the data that you know about and that is available to you. How much information you go after and collect depends on the complexity of the problem and how much time you have to spend on it. You may make a poor decision if you know too little about a problem, but you seldom err because you know too much.

In trying to define a problem, consider how it originated and why it exists. Look at its scope. More than likely, the problem consists of several subproblems that can be worked on separately. To gain a basic understanding of the problem, you must be able to answer a series of questions about it—such questions as:

- What really is the problem? Is it based on opinion or fact? Is the information you have on the problem truthful? Are bias and prejudice factors to be considered?
- Could the problem be only a symptom? Would you attack it differently if that were the case? Has the problem been defined too narrowly?
- How did the problem originate? Has it existed for some time? Is it a common problem or a unique one? What are the chances of it solving itself if you do nothing?
- Is the problem critical? How quickly must an answer be found? Should only part of the problem be tackled now?
- What will be achieved by solving the problem? Is there a goal, objective, or purpose? Are the company's plans or goals involved?

You will probably be able to answer some of these questions when you first learn of the problem. What you need now are some guidelines on how to proceed.

Guidelines for Problem Solving

First-line managers daily face problems of all sizes and degrees of difficulty. Some are so small and inconsequential that little if any analysis and study are necessary to conclude what should be done. Other problems may be difficult and time-consuming, requiring that you put a lot of time and energy into them. What is the best way to attack what appears to be a complex problem? Here are some guidelines:

1. Avoid treating the symptoms of a problem—work on its causes. In many companies, for example, much engineering and maintenance are often directed at the symptoms of a problem rather than at the problem itself, especially when equipment and machinery are involved. Too many supervisors tend to analyze symptoms rather than causes in trying to correct such problems.

2. Look beyond the simple statement of the problem. The phrasing may or may not clearly identify it. Determine whether the person giving you the problem understands it scope and what is involved. It's often a good idea to question the objective of solving a problem.

3. Be thorough in your search for facts. Consider your approach and try to avoid overlooking something. Determine whether the scope of the problem is completely defined. Check on assumptions to determine whether they are critical to the solution.

4. Don't hesitate to fully apply yourself to a problem if it will make the difference between a good solution and a mediocre one. A complex problem may require a lot of mental gymnastics plus considerable attention to details. A mechanical problem may require you to get your hands dirty. Physical involvement in a project will provide you maximum learning and experience.

5. Seek the help and advice of other people. Working by yourself on a problem that affects others is not advisable. Besides, the affected people may have opinions, ideas, or information that are pertinent. Develop a good communication style in order that questionable points may be brought into the open. Good communication fosters involvement and promotes cooperation.

6. Be rational when attacking a problem. Make sure your solution is possible with existing technology and knowledge. Use

22

common sense: You don't want to propose a complex or costly solution to a trivial problem.

7. Pause at some point during a problem-solving session to determine whether you are on the right track. Reconsider your approach. Think about what you are trying to do. This ascertainment of your position is an important step in solving the problem, in that it provides you an opportunity to uncover errors and introduce simplifications.

8. Call upon your insight and intuition. Your feelings should be given a lot of weight. Trust yourself. Have confidence that you will solve the problem and that your solution will stand the test of time.

Solving managerial problems is not easy. But some supervisors who are good at it make it look easy. They are able to do so because they take full advantage of all the resources and tools available to them. They aim for solutions that are realistic and practical. To reach these objectives, they organize their efforts, allocate their time, and fully utilize their knowledge and experience.

Staying on Top of Problems

Many first-line managers become discouraged because they are continually faced with problems requiring decisions. If you sometimes feel this way, remember that problems don't affect or interrupt your work—they *are* your work. If you didn't have problems to solve and decisions to make, you wouldn't be needed as a supervisor.

Supervisors who stay on top of problems are usually good decision makers. Their good decisions have motivated people, prevented delays, made work easier, and generally overcome the various roadblocks that keep jobs from running smoothly. The best way to stay on top of problems is to handle them as promptly as possible. Any delay aggravates matters, upsets people, and increases costs.

What are other things you must do to stay on top of problems? You must know when and where your presence is likely to be needed and try to be there. Be able to supervise several jobs at the same time and spend most of your time with your people, not at your desk. Try to split your attention among your people so that no one is neglected for a long period of time. If anybody runs into a problem, you will soon know about it. In addition, anticipate trouble and take steps to prevent it. You will have fewer problems and more time to work on those you do have.

Defining a problem well is a requisite for getting and staying on top of it. You cannot hope to find a good solution if you don't really understand the problem. Defining a problem well will sometimes reveal whether it is upstream of what you're looking at. There may be no question, for example, that buying a new machine for the factory will solve a manufacturing problem; but if you know what the true difficulty is with your existing machine, you may solve your problem with a repair or replacement of a part at much less cost. Some problems can be solved in more than one way; part of the problem is determining which solution meets your needs. In such cases, you handle the problem in the most expedient way and at the lowest cost to your company.

You can stay on top of problems much more easily if you are adept at recognizing them when they arise. It helps, also, to be aware of the similarities between problems. Research and development people are usually quite skilled at solving problems. When searching for answers to a specific problem, they often find valuable information in journals and reports on problems similar to theirs. They have learned from experience that there is no limit to the amount of information available on most problems; their real task is to take that information and apply it. Often when people start describing a problem, they will see its similarity to other problems they've had. The fact that this happens suggests that a good way to stay on top of problems is to start talking about them as soon as you learn of them. Even if you do not see a commonality with other problems you've had, perhaps your listeners will.

Solving a Problem Through Change

Before you attempt to solve a problem through change, you should ask yourself several questions:

- What exactly is to be changed?
- Is it really necessary that a change be made?
- What will be gained from the change?
- What procedure will be followed?
- What precisely will be changed as a consequence of the procedure selected?

Answering these questions before doing anything will enable you to learn of all the alternatives available to you. You will be better able to manage the change, including incorporating any worthwhile ideas suggested by others. As a result, there will be a greater probability that the decisions you make concerning the change will be good ones.

Decisions are most likely to be questioned when they concern change. If an individual believes that the consequences of a change will conflict with his or her needs, the individual will probably be under stress and develop feelings of frustration. Under such circumstances, he or she will tend to resist the change. You must be able to anticipate that resistance and estimate how great it might be. Just as important, you should also know the probable reason or reasons for the resistance. A manager who has this capability can plan and implement decisions that lessen the effect of change.

Another significant factor to be reckoned with is the extent to which people affected by a change are involved in making some of the decisions about the change. Most people like to have some control over their working environment. In addition, they gain satisfaction and a feeling of success when they are instrumental in making a change for their betterment. As a consequence, many people want to take part in making decisions that affect them directly. If this desire is fulfilled, their interest in their work increases. Furthermore, they are more likely to accept a change that they might otherwise have rejected. How they perceived the change would be altered—they would not feel they were forced into it.

There have been many cases in business and industry where personal involvement in making changes has brought about quick acceptance where resistance would otherwise have been encountered. Side benefits to management have also evolved, in that groups that participate in setting goals for themselves often ask more of themselves than their supervisors and methods or planning engineers deem practical. Jobs are completed in considerably less time than normal. More repairs are made per day when the repair crew plans the work. Yard people have worked more days when *they* decided whether or not the weather was inclement than when their supervisor made the decision. Such incidents have proved that the greater the extent of personal involvement in making decisions regarding change, the less will be the resistance to it.

Effectiveness in Handling Change

For managers to be effective in handling change, they should be concerned mainly with accomplishing a goal or objective. When managers have problems to solve, they should ask themselves, "What action will both result in the best answer to the problem and be most likely to produce the best long-term results for the company?" They should not look only for answers that would improve their own status and help their careers. Nor should they take the attitude of wanting to be sure they get credit for good decisions without being held responsible for bad ones.

Several benefits derive from a decision-making procedure that places goal accomplishment above personal and political considerations. One benefit is that a supervisor is more likely to accept others' ideas and suggestions. Another is that a supervisor tends to encourage people's involvement and participation in arriving at some of the decisions that affect the implementation of a change. A supervisor is also more apt to fully share information relative to a decision with all concerned. He or she is not tempted to seek power by withholding information. An awareness prevails as well that resistance to a change is less when people know the reason for it.

Managers who value accomplishment of an objective above their personal advancement are more willing to innovate—to try something different. They have less fear that an occasional poor decision will affect their future with the company. With many management groups, any kind of a failure, whether it be experimental or not, is typically associated with personal failure. Such managers are often reluctant to try out ideas that might not turn out well. But if the consequences of a failure are viewed as constructive and leading ultimately to better chances for success, the managers would probably be more willing to try something deviating from the norm. Such constructive perceptions of trial and error are possible when managers at all levels are concerned primarily with accomplishing a goal.

The Pitfalls of Problem Solving

Supervisors may fall into traps in the process of solving their problems and carrying out their responsibilities. The most common are: coming up with the right answer for the wrong problem, making a decision on a problem at the wrong time, and making decisions that do not result in action.

Few things are a greater waste of time than finding an answer to a problem that doesn't exist. A supervisor can look bad in the eyes of others if this happens more than once. If, for example, you as a maintenance supervisor were to decide that a major component of a machine needed to be replaced when the actual reason for the machine's failing to operate properly was misalignment, a matter easily corrected, your ability to make a sound decision on a mechanical problem would very likely be questioned.

In another decision-making area, treating imprecise data with precision and care is a trap easily fallen into. The danger here is that you may believe from your analysis that you have obtained results not capable of or susceptible to change. The average accounting department of a company your size may employ 4.4 clerks, but that doesn't mean that your department needs 4.4 calculators. Statistics provide useful guidelines, not answers.

Far too many decisions are postponed when they should be made, without the realization that postponing a decision is actually making one. On the other hand, many decisions are made before they need be. Failing to discipline an employee for repeating a serious mistake means you are condoning it. Condemning a costly machine at its first malfunction is not a logical move, especially if the difficulty is minor.

A decision without a way to implement it or control the consequences of its adoption is not an effective or even a complete decision. Such problem solving on the part of a decision maker shows impulsiveness, a lack of planning, and an inability or unwillingness to think things through.

Supervisors may make such mistakes for one or more reasons. The most probable reason is that they are not organized in their thinking and in the way they carry out their responsibilities. They act intuitively on matters that can best be handled rationally and tend to be rational about matters that require judgment. Another reason is that they spend their problem-solving time unwisely. They fail to find out what the problem is, preferring to spend time looking for the answer. Yet defining the problem correctly is both the most important and the most difficult job in making decisions. With most problems, once they are clearly defined and understood, the answer is easy.

Being practical is not an excuse to handle problems the same old tried-and-true way. A practical problem solver is a person who can successfully cope with the demands and restrictions of the real world. Imaginative solutions to problems are still part of that real world.

Insight as a Factor in Making Decisions

Managers who are good at making decisions have certain attributes that help to make them effective and successful. Insight is one of those attributes. Insight enables them to distinguish between real problems that require action and conditions or situations that are of minor importance or irrevelant to reaching their objectives.

With insight, you make sure a problem is yours before you try to handle it. You thus avoid assuming a responsibility that belongs to someone else. Properly, you should approach a problem with the attitude of what you can do and how you can help, not how you're going to use your authority to get matters straightened out. When you observe a poor situation or a problem in the office or factory that demands attention, either from you or from someone else, you become part of the decision to take action. Similarly, when you are asked for information on a problem by your boss, you are involved in its solution. Your knowledge and experience can be the vital ingredient in the success of the final decision on any problem. But your knowledge and experience will also provide you the insight into when decisions should be made.

People with insight are seldom impulsive, nor do they often make startling or radical decisions. Their perception and intuitive reasoning tell them to proceed cautiously when they are uncertain. If they feel they must act on a situation, they work for prevention rather than cure. They prefer to attack the cause of a problem rather than seek the correction of it.

Insight will enable you to avoid making important decisions when you're under pressure or stress; with insight, you will realize that you can make the best decision when you are calm and have time to think. You seek out problems rather than waiting for them to seek you out.

How do you gain insight if you don't have it? Here are several ways to go about acquiring it:

- Become knowledgeable about your department, company, and industry.
- Know what the standard procedure is for handling certain problems.
- Be adept at setting priorities and understand the relationships between planning, scheduling, and executing.
- Try to be creative and innovative by finding new and unique solutions to problems.
- Know your people and their capabilities; persuade and motivate them.
- See that your decisions are acted upon and carried out. Always follow up.

Decisiveness

Probably no question bothers a supervisor more than the simple "Should I or shouldn't I?" Yet supervisors must choose between the two courses of action many times each day. Reluctance to make a decision is a common human weakness, but what holds you back, more often than not, isn't lack of wisdom but timidity. Many people in leadership positions lack enough self-confidence and assertiveness to take action when they face a problem where a decision should be made. This unwillingness to act results in nothing being done or in permitting those who are willing to act to take over.

You may find yourself in such a position many times in your career. How aggressive you are at such times may determine how high you rise in management with your company. Boldness is a requisite of the successful manager.

A first-line manager is expected by his or her company to use good judgment in carrying out the responsibilities of the position. Using good judgment means making sound decisions and making them at opportune times. Effective supervisors are decisive. When making decisions, they provide assurance and confidence to subordinates to go ahead with their work without fear.

What is meant by being decisive? When you are decisive, you do more than merely give an opinion—you act on that opinion. Decisiveness is a willingness to commit yourself and to follow up on your conviction. The person who takes a firm stand on an issue and starts the ball rolling toward resolving it is said to be decisive.

How do you acquire the skill of being decisive? Gain insight and develop determination if you want to be decisive. Welcome problems and have the confidence to solve them. Be willing to decide something. Reluctance to make a decision can handicap you because people on the job expect their supervisors to be decisive and in control. Workers become fearful, uneasy, and even unwilling to go ahead with a job when they sense that their supervisor is unsure of himself or herself. A decisive manager commands respect and gets action.

Being decisive in handling your responsibilities requires that you make minor decisions promptly. By disposing of them as quickly as possible you will have more time to spend on problems that are really important. Be solid and firm when you make a decision. Don't be half-sure or leave any doubt about your intentions. Put aside any thoughts that you might make a mistake. Such thinking weakens your resolution to be decisive. Also, forget the alternative once you make a decision. There is no sense in wasting time thinking about what you could or should have done.

To be decisive, you should approach a problem in a definite way. Your course of action should involve several steps to enable you to make the best decision possible under the circumstances. To start with, you must study and analyze the problem thoroughly. Recognize that any decision you make depends on how much you know about it. You may make a poor decision if you know too little, so learn about the situation, how it developed, the issue involved, and what you need to accomplish with your decision.

Consider the possible decisions that could be made. Is your usual answer to this type of problem the best, or must you look for a different approach? Evaluate all possible alternatives. Narrow your choices to the best one by weighing the outcome you could expect from each. Will your decision solve the problem or accomplish your objective? Is the solution fair to all concerned? Is your answer partial or temporary? Will it handle the entire problem now?

Take action on your decision and plan to follow up after a reasonable period of time. You've been decisive if you've not procrastinated along the way.

Delegating Responsibility and Decisions

A basic principle of organization is that responsibility should be delegated to the lowest level in the organization that is capable of satisfactory performance. If you have demonstrated to your boss that you are capable of making certain decisions, he or she should delegate those problems and issues to you. But this is not to say that you sometimes don't accept a responsibility on your own when the boss is absent and make a decision that he or she normally would. Unless you are unusually capable, you're bound to make some mistakes. Your boss should understand and give you some growing room; in that way, you'll learn and gradually become a better decision maker.

The only way to learn to be decisive is to make decisions. If the penalties for making errors are too high, either for you or for your boss, then you may avoid taking on new responsibilities and the decision making that goes with them. Good decision makers, however, don't evolve from such situations.

There are those in management who may argue that you can't expect certain people to assume responsibility. That's generally not true. Most first-line managers are capable of taking on a lot more responsibility than their superiors give them credit for.

Often what appears to be indecisiveness is really a lack of responsibility, which is irresponsibility. We retreat to irresponsibility because of lack of confidence and because of stress. Taking on responsibility is the best way to become a good decision maker and move up the hierarchy of your company.

Because you have participated in making a decision, should you always be motivated and committed to carrying it out? That depends on whether you accept the principle that participation is a motivator. If you do not want to do a particular job yet are asked to participate in a decision concerning that job, a decision contrary to your opinion will make you unhappy. Not only may you now be required to do a job that you don't want to do, but you may also have to do it under pressure from both your peers and management. Along the same lines, if you contribute to a decision on a matter about which you know nothing, but your advice is taken, you may now feel a commitment and motivation to carry out the wrong decision. Participation in decision making commits you. But the pertinent questions are: To what are you committed, and why do you commit yourself?

When a Decision Should Not Be Made

Supervisors may sometimes be overimpressed by the apparent importance and urgency of making a decision. They would fare better in such cases if they paused to consider the situation at length. There are many occasions on the job when it is not wise to make an immediate decision. For one thing, if the decision can be postponed, it may turn out that it is not necessary to make it. Hesitating is particularly wise when supervisors are under stress. Effective supervisors resist being forced into making decisions without taking time to think about them beforehand. Of course, occasionally a very quick decision must be made, such as when an emergency situation exists.

When a first-line manager is pressed for a decision, he or she should first decide whether a temporary or interim one would suffice. While such a decision may not provide an entirely satisfactory solution to the problem, it usually alleviates a sticky situation and gives the manager time to work out a solution that is acceptable to everyone involved. However, there are instances when stalling for time may aggravate a situation. Putting off a decision on a safety matter, for example, may leave the door open for another accident. A delay in answering a union grievance could cause a drop in the productivity of a work group. You should always study a situation carefully to determine what effect a delay might have; decide what steps should be taken immediately and what matters can be deferred. Only after doing this can you estimate how long your final or complete decision can be put off.

Being decisive is usually to you advantage and a behavior pattern for which you will be admired. It suggests that you are in control and willing to be responsible. Nevertheless, there are times when it's better not to decide something. Here are a few such cases:

• Don't act when the decision you are about to make does not jibe with your intuition. Check your hunch, particularly when you're going to make a decision involving people; a hunch may be better than logic in such cases.

• Don't decide something when you know you don't have all the facts. Continue to investigate and study the problem without making up your mind. You will then be prepared for the time when you *must* make the decision.

• Delay a decision when you're not sure of its consequences. Situations and conditions change with time, as does how people see them. Waiting will enable you to prepare to reverse yourself in the event the consequences of your ultimate decision are not favorable.

• Don't make a decision when other viewpoints that you don't yet have could affect its acceptability.

• Stall for time when other people are trying to force your decision. There's a good chance that they may be pushing you for what they can get out of it, not for what you will. They may eventually show their hand, enabling you to view the problem in a different light.

Group Decision Making

Group decision making is becoming more and more common in many companies. In some cases, committees make decisions. In others, special task forces are assigned to a problem; and in still others, informal discussions are conducted among management personnel, including supervisors. Consensus is the key to successful group decision making. All concerned parties must agree on a decision. If all the people who are responsible for implementing it are in agreement, they will be motivated to make the decision a successful one.

Although first-line managers are generally left to themselves to make decisions in carrying out the functions of their job, when an other-than-routine decision has to be made, they may consult with others to get information and explore different viewpoints. In one industry, a group of supervisors periodically get together with their superior to make decisions concerning the department. With participative management becoming popular, more and more supervisors and workers meet informally to discuss problems and reach decisions. Such meetings are good, in that in addition to helping participants decide what is to be done and how to do it, they help bring people together for a team effort. They also make each worker feel that his or her opinion is valued and that he or she is contributing to make the company grow and prosper. As for whether groups make better decisions than individuals, there are both advantages and disadvantages to group decision making.

Perhaps the most rewarding advantage of group decision making is that the group offers additional resources. People from varied disciplines can supply all sorts of information and ideas, and they have differing viewpoints to express. With such a variety of opinions and experiences, groups can often present more alternatives than could any single individual. Groups may also add a creative touch to the solution of a problem. While one member may be very creative and offer a good idea, someone else may suggest something that sparks ideas in others' minds. Complementing and coordinating ideas can lead to better solutions than any individual could develop by himself or herself. Such interaction is the basis of brainstorming as a procedure for solving problems. Greater acceptance of decisions is an outgrowth of group action, and more effective implementation is a consequence of it. When people participate in making a decision, they tend to be committed and motivated to accept it and put it into effect.

Where a decision can be made better by the contribution of

several minds, that is how it should be made. A good case illustrating this is the work of the safety committee in the factory or office, whose primary purpose is to bring about safe conditions and practices among the workers. Another is the suggestion committee, which promotes and judges ideas and innovations.

However, don't be misled into believing that group decision making is preferred over other ways to solve business problems—it is far from perfect. Although some of its weaknesses cannot be avoided, others can be attributed to ineffective functioning of the group. For example, groups frequently take more time to make decisions than individuals do. An individual can get information, analyze it, consider alternatives, and decide much faster. No time is consumed in discussing the problem at length with other people when a single individual makes a decision. However, implementation may take longer. The supervisor must tell people of his or her decision and persuade others to accept it. When a group makes a decision, the decision-making time is longer, but communication time and persuasion time are short. Thus, with some decisions, it takes just as long to get action on a decision made by a group.

Groups formed for the purpose of making decisions must contend with other inherent weaknesses. For instance, members often try very hard to be friendly to one another and to avoid conflicts. Such efforts reduce the group's ability to be realistic in evaluating alternatives. Getting along well together becomes more important than making good decisions. Because of this strong desire for harmony, omissions of duty and responsibility may prevail. Also, where action and judgment of a group are limited to a single function, the group's decisions may be weak and ineffective. In addition, such groups may be formed with a secret objective—to share the blame if anything goes wrong. Further, a group may not consider all the possible alternatives, nor may it thoroughly study the initially preferred decision for risks and drawbacks. Outside information may not be sought; and there is a tendency to go along with the group's opinions; conflicting opinions may be ignored. But since group decision making has much to offer management, there should be no thought of abandoning it simply because it has some imperfections. Rather, management should try to improve the procedures so that maximum benefits can be achieved based on the method's advantages.

A common problem is that the size of the group is not right for the task it is to perform. If the group is too large, some members do not find it easy to contribute. Yet if the group is too small, not enough opinions and views are represented. Then, too, groups, regardless of their size, need someone to act as a leader. The most effective leader is one who is adept in conducting meetings and getting participants to contribute. A good leader can often overcome the drawbacks of poor group size.

The leader, who may be a supervisor, is responsible for the agenda and the problems to be resolved. He or she should do considerable planning and goal setting before the group convenes. It pays if the leader is a flexible individual so that he or she can convey to the group the need for innovation and creativity in finding solutions to problems and in settling issues. Differences of opinion are expected in group meetings. This is to the good because disagreements can actually help to improve the group's decisions. The greater the range of information and opinion, the more likely the group will make good decisions.

Strategy for Problem Solving

Managers are better able to know what to do about a problem if they can relate it to one of their particular functions or responsibilities. By doing this, they more easily recognize the factors involved and the questions that have been answered. They can then develop a strategy for attacking the problem. The following checklists have been prepared to help you with the problems you face and enable you to make better decisions regarding them. Recognize, however, that they are very limited and are intended only to serve as a guide.

Search Problems

How to recognize the situation	• You are looking for something. • You are seeking opportunities. • You want to learn why an error is occurring. • You want to uncover unsafe conditions.

Typical complications and roadblocks	• You are not aware of who has such information. • The files are not up to date. • Company policy forbids releasing the information for security reasons. • Management doesn't recognize the need for a computer.
Suggested approach and strategy	• Enlist the help of the company's records center. • Call people who previously worked in the department. • Consider hiring a consultant. • Research the literature for how others have handled that or similar problems.

Waiting-Line Problems

How to recognize the situation	• People at the storeroom window. • Trucks to be loaded or unloaded. • Customers at a checkout counter. • Jobs for a skilled craftsperson. • Mail to be answered. • Telephone calls to be returned. • Components awaiting final assembly.
Typical complications and roadblocks	• Loss of productivity because of idleness. • Inability to meet shipping schedules. • Impatient customers leave. • Orders lost because they are not acknowledged by phone or mail. • Storage space problems. • High inventories. • Some waiting lines are last-in, first-out instead of the usual first-in, first-out.
Suggested approach and strategy	• Weigh the service provided against the seriousness of the delay. • Change policy to eliminate lines entirely. • Temporarily assign more people to check out the job. • Use an operations research technique to work out the answer to the problem.

Information Problems

How to recognize the situation
- You need information in order to take proper action.
- Your boss has asked you a question you can't answer.
- The accounting department has asked you for costs of your operation.
- You must make out an accident report.
- Your progress report to the boss is due.

Typical complications and roadblocks
- Your primary source of information is sick.
- The boss is in a hurry.
- The cost department has not tabulated your costs.
- There are no witnesses to an accident.
- You will have to communicate with many people to learn the status of current projects.

Suggested approach and strategy
- Assign priorities to each of the information demands you must satisfy. Work on top-priority jobs first.
- Determine which system or organization can provide you the required information.
- Consider which information source will be best for each and every problem.
- Make requests for information as soon as you learn of the need for it.
- Determine means of confirming data and information.

Control Problem

How to recognize the situation
- You want to be in charge to get jobs done.
- You need to know when you must make a decision.
- You must determine what kind of decision should be made.
- You must put your decision into effect.

Typical complications and roadblocks
- You don't have authority over the person who needs to be controlled.

- A control mechanism is not available for your particular problem.
- Change is taking place so rapidly that any control you attempt may soon be obsolete.

Suggested approach and strategy	• Plan how you will control the system or situation. • Decide what you will achieve through the control. • Provide a way of measuring what is done. • Know what you must do to correct a deviation and keep in control.

Labor and Material Allocation Problems

How to recognize the situation	• You have resources to distribute or allocate among competing demands. • Your responsibility is to allocate your resources in the best interests of the company.
Typical complications and roadblocks	• Your labor resource is limited. • Key individuals are absent. • The supply of material is limited. • Material needs to be relocated to point of use. • Too broad an allocation of resources reduces the extent to which any particular demand can be satisfied. • Too narrow an allocation limits the number of demands that can be satisfied.
Suggested approach and strategy	• Establish good relations with other departments to facilitate the exchange of labor on request. • Keep current on materials inventories and sources of supply. • Optimize achievement of desired objectives by the most effective allocation of resources among competing demands.

Replacement Problems

How to recognize the situation	• There is a need to replace resources such as facilities, equipment, machinery, and tools.
	• You have the responsibility of deciding how to replace those resources most effectively and efficiently.
Typical complications and roadblocks	• Buy or build?
	• Lease or buy?
	• Trade agreements.
	• Guarantees and warranties.
	• Replace only components or the entire machine?
	• Replace other than failed components when the machine is being repaired?
	• Early replacement increases investment and capital value.
	• Late replacement may cause delays and increases the cost of maintenance and repair.
Suggested approach and strategy	• Investigate alternative courses of action, considering cost, life of replacement, and ease of accomplishment.
	• Balance costs of early replacement against late replacement.
	• Minimize the sum of all replacement costs: investment, maintenance and repair, equipment and machine downtime, and safety and housekeeping.
	• Use an operations research technique to make decisions relating to component parts replacement.

Inventory Problems

How to recognize the situation	• Inventory of either raw materials, operating supplies, or finished goods is too high or too low.
	• Savings can be realized from large-quantity purchases.

- There is a best time to order some items.
- Inventory is needed to meet future demand.

Typical complications and roadblocks

- Capital tied up in inventory.
- Insufficient storage area for high inventory.
- Too much inventory means excessive carrying costs (cost of storing, cost of money, cost of spoilage or damage in storage, cost of obsolescence, and so on).
- Too little inventory results in down time of productive equipment or delays in production.
- Distribution and relocation are more of a problem with high inventories.

Suggested approach and strategy

- Balance too much inventory against too little. Minimize the sum of carrying costs plus outage costs.
- Use the economic order quantity formulas.
- Request that vendors stock material.
- Use the computer for materials management (purchasing, receiving, storing, ordering, accounting, and paying for materials).

Chapter Three

Factors
that Influence
Decisions

Business theory, backed up by tradition, dictates that decision making be assigned to the lowest competent level in an organization. There are good reasons for this. The closer a decision maker is to a problem or situation requiring action, the quicker the decision can be made. Besides, if too many decisions are passed upward, higher-level management will be overburdened and those in the lower levels will have little opportunity to show initiative.

What is the lowest competent level in a company? Generally, it is the lowest level at which a jobholder has both the access to the information and data needed to make the decision and the incentive and skill to weigh and consider all the factors. Thus, if a supervisor is put in charge of a manufacturing process and is provided with labor, equipment, and material, he or she may be said to have all the resources needed to operate the process. The supervisor will be judged on how efficiently the process is operated and how productive his or her people are. The supervisor is not, however, competent to decide how much of the money the company has available for investment should be spent on that process instead of on other capital ventures. Only upper management is competent to make such decisions. Often the center of decision-making activity may be determined by the extent to which the outcome will affect profits. If a decision is not likely to affect profits very much one way or the other, management may not be overly concerned about who in the company makes the decision or at what level it is made.

The Risk

Making a decision always entails some risk for both the first-line manager and his or her company. Except in routine matters, the consequences of a decision are seldom entirely predictable. If the outcome is unfavorable, the company may lose money or its reputation may suffer; the manager may miss out on a raise or a promotion—or even lose his or her job if the decision was a really bad one.

Although management experts say that a supervisor will be successful if more than 50 percent of his or her decisions are good, such statements are misleading. Different decisions have widely varying impacts. It is usually impossible to determine in advance just how wide-ranging the impact of a particular decision will be. However, there are some tests that a supervisor can apply to predict how great the impact may be if the outcome is unfavorable.

Risk is the term used to express the probability of a project's success or failure. Low risk is usually associated with projects for which costs and benefits can be calculated on the basis of significant experience and reliable data. High risk, in comparison, is usually associated with projects for which costs and benefits are difficult to determine precisely. This is often due to uncertainty about the data because of insufficient experience.

The length of time during which the impact of the decision will be felt may be important. Some decisions can be quickly reversed if their outcomes prove unfavorable. The company may have to live with others until their effect wears off or the company provides compensation in some manner. It is not always easy to determine how long the effects of a decision will last. Although an incompetent higher-level manager or supervisor may quickly be discharged for poor performance, he or she may have done great longer-term harm to the department or company by alienating customers or by causing a high turnover of people who were important to the company's growth and welfare.

Risks vary from low to very high, and you take a risk with just about every decision you make. It stands to reason, then, that you should avoid making a decision, if possible, when the risks are high; prefer to make decisions where the potential for gain is great. But how do you know when such conditions exist? Mathematicians say you can know by using Pareto's law. The theory behind this concept is based on the fact that, on the average, 80 percent of the results in a given situation can be attributed to 20 percent of the possible causes. For example, 80 percent of the complaints from your people are filed by 20 percent of them, and 80 percent of the mistakes made on the job are attributable to 20 percent of the workers. Astute managers concentrate their efforts on the vital few problems, not the trivial many. You should do the same in deciding what risks to take. Ironically, there's a risk in not taking risks. If you don't think positively and optimistically, you tend to become negative and overly cautious. If you don't try something new or strange, you may soon find yourself in a rut, so to speak, and never thereafter try to better yourself and get ahead.

Taking risks means different things to different people. What one man sees as a threat because he thinks he will fail, another man sees as a challenge because he thinks he will succeed. There will always be some amount of risk you must accept if you are going to do anything, including leaving your home to go to work as well as selecting your lunch menu. The many decisions you make during the day must always tip the scales in favor of gain rather than loss and being successful rather than failing.

Contending with Risks

Risk taking in business cannot be avoided. Any particular decision can always be wrong, since no first-line manager ever has the time necessary to acquire all the facts bearing upon it. For instance, a supervisor is never sure what the labor union will do about a decision he or she makes. There will always be a risk, too, that machinery failure or a utility outage will interrupt a production process, delaying a shipment to a customer. Managers must face up to the existence of risks in making operating decisions and do their best to offset those risks in order to minimize their influence on operating results. Here are some guidelines to help you take risks effectively:

• Always have a goal in mind when taking a risk. A risk taken without a purpose is foolhardy. Not only that, but it's hard to tell when you are winning or losing without a goal to shoot for. A timetable also helps, as does a schedule, because they provide direction and assurance that your plan is working. Anything that aids your ability to predict lessens the risk. Similarly, if you list everything that can go wrong and why, you'll be aware of problems sooner because you'll be looking for them.

• Recognize that you will always have problems involving risk. Intend to handle them your way as much as you can because you'll be in a better position to dictate the outcome. Be serious about the risks you take, especially when the stakes are high. You intend to accomplish something when you risk. If you don't intend to succeed, you intend to fail.

• Be realistic. Some roadblocks you can hurdle, some you can't. Know when you would never act and when you would act without question. Decide how you could compromise in the interests of safety, but recognize that if you are looking for a totally safe risk, there is no such thing.

• Consider what is the best effort you are capable of making and don't plan on being able to do more than that. Ask questions if you're in doubt. It's better to appear stupid than to make a big mistake. Aim to succeed and gain from your efforts.

• Don't take a risk just to prove to yourself that you can succeed. This is hazardous risking and totally unnecessary. You may get away with it a few times if you are lucky but will suffer when you eventually fail. Also, don't rush into something. Take enough time to be sure you know what you're doing. Imagine yourself in the position you're thinking about taking. Figure out what you would do or say. Merely setting your mind to work on the problem is often all you need to become familiar with what you fear.

• Don't take a risk because of anger, guilt, hurt, or depression. Emotional risks should be taken only with emotional problems. If you are angry, you can risk expressing it, but you cannot risk hitting someone or destroying something. In other words, don't act out your feelings. Avoid beating a dead horse—you can tell when something is lost. Let a bad situation end. Don't prolong it.

• Be decisive. Once you have decided that the risk is worthy and the time is right, act. Delaying at this moment is dangerous. Hesitation is not in the interests of safety. Although taking risks of any type may not appeal to you, realize that nothing great was ever achieved without risk.

• Give people credit for helping you to reach your decision and take the risk. You need all the friends you can get when you risk; your best friends are those who have already given you help. Friends who feel slighted or neglected can cause you more trouble than enemies.

Positive Thinking

The type of decision you make is at least partly determined by whether you are a positive or negative thinker. Many first-line managers have been persuaded and trained to think positively. Yet in order to be decisive and make good decisions, they have to learn to face reality—there are both unpleasant and distasteful decisions that must be made.

You can't be a wishful thinker when you make decisions. Positive thinking is an aid if you don't let it interfere with reality because it can motivate you to see an opportunity when you face a problem. Positive thinking leads you to seek the best in going after your goals while allowing for roadblocks and setbacks. Positive thinking can be a big help in being decisive and in implementing a decision. If you think about the good that will come from a decision, you will be encouraged to take the steps necessary to bring it about. You can be spurred to perform a difficult or distasteful task if you know the outcome will be fruitful and rewarding.

However, if positive thinking causes you to be impractical, then it is more likely to lead to a bad decision than a good one. This can happen in an organization where goals are set too high and no one wants to say they can't be reached. As a consequence, many of the decisions are overambitious. When you make a decision concerning only yourself, you are not as likely to ignore reality, but you can still get in trouble. The way out is to use positive thinking *after* you have made a decision, not before.

Positive people concentrate on what they can do and center their attention on the task instead of the reasons why something may fail. If you are convinced that you cannot make a good decision, chances are you won't. This does not imply, though, that the reverse is always true—that if you believe you can make good decisions, you will. Self-confidence certainly helps. Given two supervisors with similar and equal abilities—one who always identifies the reasons why something cannot possibly be done and one who approaches a problem positively—higher-level managers are more inclined to give tougher assignments and ultimately more responsibility to the latter. A supervisor who tries will get ahead much faster than one who holds back when a difficult problem must be solved.

First-line managers in particular should be positive thinkers. The manager who comes across positively with people combats the "it doesn't matter" attitude. You should try not to let such an attitude exist or grow with your people. Keep them aware of the worth of what they are doing. Thinking negatively turns people off. It discourages them and kills their enthusiasm. A depressing aspect of such thinking is that only the bad side of events is seen; that, plus the tendency to inflate the negative, often makes a situation appear much worse than it really is.

Some employees seem to be negatively oriented. They can always find reasons why things can't be done, why your idea won't work, why anything new or different doesn't stand a chance. Such employees like things the way they are and don't want to see them changed. While this type of thinking is most commonly found with older people, no one is immune to it. Inexperienced or experienced, novice or pro, new hire or long service—anyone can fall into the trap of being negative. Your job as a supervisor is to turn such individuals around. When they say something won't work, assign them the job of discovering what will. You'll get them to think more positively and respect people who make constructive suggestions.

The secret of getting your people to think positively is to convince them that such thinking is best for them. Positive thinkers get more enjoyment and satisfaction from life because they become involved with more things; they are active and interested in what is going on about them. Coupled with their optimism is a drive that causes things to work out better for them.

Positive thinking on the part of leaders regarding their subordinates makes the subordinates feel good and want to do a better job. Many times it goes beyond that. The worker whose boss is sincere and sees the good in his or her performance will be more satisfied with the job and will actually do better work because of that satisfaction.

Human Factors

Although a first-line manager may not be aware of it, the human element is a factor in just about every decision he or she makes. In addition, every decision maker has personal objectives related to his or her job as well as to his or her life as a whole; these objectives affect the person's decisions. Self-approval is an essential requirement for being satisfied with a decision. Simply gaining rewards is not enough—you must be able to live with yourself. Heredity and the environment are also factors in determining your effectiveness in decision making, but they are far from being major influences. You can learn to make good decisions, since the act of decision making is a type of behavior. The decisions you have made and are making reflect your judgment and experience. Except for highly experienced decision makers, most people could do much better than they are now doing.

It is generally true that every decision is based on five elements: facts, knowledge, experience, analysis, and judgment. Although some of these elements play a more important role than others in enabling an individual to make a good decision, in the absence of any of them, a decision maker must call upon certain substitutes. For example, data and information readily fill in for facts; advice and recommendations serve for knowledge; experimentation and trial take the place of experience; and hunch and intuition can be relied upon to some extent for analysis. However, there is no substitute for judgment.

Judgment is often looked upon as an intuitive reaction to

questions demanding an immediate answer. People who make decisions without recourse to analysis and evaluation are relying on judgment for their response. Judgment is based on experience and improves in quality through experience. A person who has experienced something more than once finds it easier to make a good decision relative to it than the person who faces the particular situation for the first time.

Good decision makers try to be, and generally are, objective. To be so, they must understand their own prejudices and their orientation; they must compensate for these personal characteristics in making decisions that are for the greatest good of the company. It is not always the case that supervisors' goals and their company's goals are similar. Some first-line managers may become so wrapped up with the objectives of their own departments that they fail to consider the parent company. Decisions they make may be so tinged with personal motives as to be inconsistent with company goals. This practice may continue when they move up in the company, in that they may still act and react as they did when they were first-line managers, and their decisions may reflect this weakness.

The human side of decision making is frequently displayed in the fear that many first-line managers have of making decisions. This often arises from mistakes and errors made early in their careers, especially if they were criticized for them. Intelligent managers realize that they cannot always be right and that it is better to be wrong once in a while than to fail to make needed decisions and so get nothing done. Supervisors can afford a few bad decisions as long as their good ones outweigh them. If people use the tools available to them and objectively evaluate the alternatives, it is highly likely that most of their decisions will be good ones.

The use of pride is a very strong tool in handling a person who is emotional and unwilling to accept your decision. It has a calming effect, in that it makes the person feel important and worthwhile. One of the differences between a good and an average trainer in the office or factory is how the good trainer gains the confidence and interest of the trainee. Pride in previous learning, brought out by the trainer, elicits greater effort in future learning. Through appealing to a person's pride, you can put him or her in a frame of mind to be especially receptive to a request you may make. The person's mood becomes agreeable and cooperative since you have demonstrated that your thinking is right when you complimented him or her. When you appeal to a person's pride, though, you must be sincere. Your method of complimenting the person must be honest. You are dishonest when you exaggerate the worth or value of a deed or when you have your facts wrong while professing to be knowledgeable. Honest compliments ring true. They are expressed simply, to the point, and without emotion.

Being satisfied with and liking their work are two of people's most important needs. People gain satisfaction from their work by being able to participate in determining the job's content and the way the work is done and by being assigned certain responsibilities. Employees need to be able to grow on the job. They can learn and gain experience when their supervisor gives them challenging work, when the job demands attention, and when the work is interesting. All of these conditions are usually controlled by first-line managers.

For example, the supervisor of two pipe fitters in an industrial plant assigns them work in a certain manner. When the supervisor is given a work order to install a piping system, he or she first has a sketch made of the general layout. It shows only the site of the installation and the system requirements, such as source of water supply, line size, and type of material to be used. He or she hands the sketch to the pipe fitters with the remark, "See me if you have any questions." The pipe fitters have a challenge requiring their knowledge and skill on such matters as routing the line, valving, bypasses, gauges, strainers, unions, and the like that should be put into the system. This makes their work interesting. Moreover, they are rightfully proud when they view their finished work and when they see the system in operation. They tackle the supervisor's next assignment eagerly and willingly. If you are the supervisor of a person or persons whose job entails many details, try leaving some of the details unspecified when you hand out your assignments. You'll have more satisfied people at the end of each workday and probably higher-quality work performed every day.

Your decision making on how to give work assignments will be simplified if you are a believer in praise as a motivator. Most workers need periodic praise, whether they are aware of it or not, and everyone occasionally needs to hear that he or she has done a good job. Praise arouses feelings of competence and capability, which, in turn, motivate and lead to further good performance. Two unfortunate things happen when managers fail to praise their people. First, they risk that workers deserving of praise will not continue doing a good job for lack of encouragement. Second, they do not take advantage of the chance to reward someone, an act that is always pleasant to perform. In both instances, the opportunity to motivate someone is missed.

An illustration of how praise pays off is the case of a supervisor who used it to motivate an office machine repairman. The fellow was having trouble getting along with his peers and his supervisor. He didn't seem interested in the job and was frequently seen wandering around the office, talking to the clerks and taking unscheduled coffee breaks. Although the supervisor docked his pay after one such incident, his behavior didn't change. One day an urgent repair job came up. One of the advanced duplicating machines had broken down, and the office would be seriously handicapped if it were not quickly repaired. The supervisor saw the opportunity to help the mechanic as well as the company. Calling the mechanic to the office, the supervisor told him that the maintenance department needed to put its best person on the repair since skill was required and the job had to be done as soon as possible. The supervisor added that he knew the mechanic could do the job better and faster than any mechanic the company had. The repairman jumped at the opportunity to demonstrate his skill and did an excellent job. Today he is no longer shunned by his peers and is much more productive. He responded when offered praise instead of criticism. This approach on the part of his supervisor motivated him and was the basic reason for his change in behavior.

Appreciation is another tool that is of great help to supervisors in getting people to accept decisions and respond productively. You can see the look of appreciation on someone's face when you tell the person that you have confidence in him or her. Also, by telling people that you appreciate what they have done in the past, you motivate them to respond with more of the same. In talking with one of your people, mention something noteworthy the person has achieved. Periodically let him or her know, too, what good work means to you. For example, say, "I appreciate the extra time you put in on that job. It really helped our department. Thanks."

Appreciation can also be shown through public recognition by the news media. It can make quite an impact, particularly when attention is called to the fact that a job was done under favorable conditions, such as time, location, or weather. Call the editor of your company publication or the local newspaper when you have some interesting or unusual accomplishment by one of your people to report.

One of the major problems of supervisors is motivating people to do their jobs willingly and efficiently. How do you get people to want to be more productive and efficient? What does it take to make people like their work? Here are a few suggestions on making decisions that concern getting things done through others:

• Learn what your people want from their jobs. If you wish to know why people behave as they do, look into each person's background and experience. Knowing someone's likes and dislikes will tell you how to motivate him or her. One person may take pride in working quickly, while another is more concerned with being thorough. One person may prefer to work by himself, while another likes to work with a team. Get to know each worker under your supervision.

• Give people credit for good work. Recognition is more important to many people than salary or working conditions. People want to be recognized for their work. Safety and good housekeeping awards can do this in the factory and office. Making the biggest sale or the most sales is a good reason for giving an award for field work. To be most effective, a first-line manager should make an award when most of the employees are together, such as at a coffee break or during lunch hour. Some companies may hold a dinner at which the main event is the awarding of prizes for outstanding performance. The posting of letters and newspaper clippings on the company bulletin board is also a way of informing employees of deeds and feats of their fellow workers. Suggestion awards given out in group gatherings often accomplish more in motivating people than the money itself. Supervisors should tell their people when they have done a good job and when they have done more than was asked of them. Everyone likes sincere praise.

• Communicate with your people. People on the job like to have friendly conversations with others, and such conversations need not always be on matters relating to the work. They especially appreciate friendly remarks by their supervisors. You can inspire your people by talking with them. Many times people lack motivation simply because they do not know how to fit into the group, what part they will play. First-line managers should tell their people what they expect of them and how they will benefit from what is going to be done. Most employees like to "know the score" and be "in the know" about what is going on, even if they are not directly involved. Communicating involves more than just talking to people; it is a two-way street. You must also listen when they talk to you. Observation alone is not enough for understanding people. When you talk to a person, both of you must be interested in learning.

• Be enthusiastic. Show that you are excited about your involvement with various projects and jobs. If you make your decisions with enthusiasm, people will see that you are eager to make progress and get work done; they will tend to be that way, too. An optimistic outlook also helps to sell your ideas and ways of handling the work. A good attitude simplifies the task of motivating other people. Be positive in your statements and actions. The will to win is often the only difference between a winner and a loser.

Personal Factors

Supervisors are people, and people have emotions. Psychologists say that most of us are emotional, not rational, much of the time. Yet to be a good decision maker, it is necessary to be rational—to make decisions based on facts. We all have our prejudices, quirks, and hang-ups. When these characteristics distort our thinking, we should try to get rid of them in order to be fair and just in our decisions. Wise managers deal with facts, and their brains react accordingly.

If you want to get more out of your job, including the making of good decisions, then you should go further than increasing your technical competence. Personal success depends on mental growth and a continual striving toward emotional maturity. Stable and mature supervisors see themselves and others realistically. They resolve conflicts and solve problems with confidence, considering both matters as challenges, not misfortunes. Build on your successes and learn from your mistakes. Don't let criticism get to you and weaken your confidence. As a decision maker, you're a perfect target. Expect criticism occasionally and recognize it for what it is. If censure isn't valid, find out what's behind it. Envy can be ignored, but if the criticizer lacks knowledge, you need to do a better job of communication. If many people criticize you, it means that something is wrong. Look into the situation and do what you can to correct it.

An emotionally mature person shows the attribute in many ways. You can demonstrate that you have this admirable human quality by:

- Being willing to accept responsibility for the mistakes of your people.
- Cheerfully sharing credit for a good decision with those who helped you.
- Helping people more and criticizing them less.
- Having the courage to take an unpopular stand on an issue.
- Being willing to concede that you could be wrong, even when convinced you are right.

To be rated high on sincerity, you must be ready and willing to support your people at any time. Call each person by his or her name; this technique helps give support that is positive. You show no support or negative support when you are impatient, favor one worker over another, and find examples only of poor work. Whenever you place your self-interest above that of your department, you issue an unmistakable message that you're not interested in the welfare of your people. Better that you help them to do good work and be as prompt be in responding to their requests as you expect them to be in responding to yours.

The personal lives of subordinates should not be your concern; in fact, they are none of your business. However, there is an exception: when the personal affairs of a subordinate affect his or her performance or the reputation and integrity of the company. It is a first-line manager's responsibility to handle such a situation promptly. Every subordinate must understand that no company can employ anyone, no matter how valuable, whose personal conduct is injurious to its business and reputation. Even though supervisors should not become involved in the personal lives of their people, they can demonstrate a genuine interest in them and their families. When people are happy with their work, home becomes a place where they find understanding, encouragement, and support for their efforts. The supervisor often tries to foster such an environment by being friendly but never intimate. Nothing a supervisor says or does must cloud the fact that he or she is in charge on the job and represents management.

Pressure and Stress

Today's rapid and sometimes radical change in life-styles, emphasis on productivity, and concern for high costs have put pressures on all of us. We feel we must do a better job, accomplish more, and keep costs down. You may feel the pressure of these and other demands, and it could affect how you make decisions. One way to handle pressure is to discuss your situation with someone. Talking it out helps, in that your mind finds relief almost as if you were transferring some of the pressure to your listener. Such a discussion has another benefit, in that often the person you talk to can help you with your problem.

Consider the possibility that you may be regarding a particular situation as worse than it really is. How important is it that the problem be solved immediately? Must your decision be made today? Do other people think that action on your part is as urgent and necessary as you do? Often you can take pressure off yourself by conceding to someone or by letting something happen that you were trying to prevent. Reconsider your position. You may find a flaw in your thinking and discover that you are entirely right in what you are trying to do. There is also the possibility that if you yield a bit, other people may, too. Cooperation and enthusiasm can do wonders to relieve pressure. Give someone a break, and you'll get one in return. Pressure can be tough, but there are numerous ways to contend with it. You'll make better decisions by learning and adopting them.

Coping with stress is an inevitable part of working as a first-line manager. Since you cannot live a life completely free of stress, you must develop ways of dealing with it. You must learn to manage stress so as to avoid the physical and mental difficulties you might otherwise have to endure.

The intensity of stress varies with three factors: your personal vulnerability at a given point in time, the environment in which you are operating, and the nature of a particular demand on you. Doctors, in general, agree with this and have developed suggestions about how to live with stress based on these ideas. If you feel that you are frequently subject to stress. it will pay you to consider and take their advice. Here are some of the techniques they say you can successfully use to fight stress:

• Talk out your problems. Problems often seem much worse when you alone carry their burden. Talking to a trusted friend, another supervisor, or your spouse can help you to put matters in a different perspective and lighten the load. Sometimes another person will point out a different side to your problem, and thus, a solution. Talking out a problem is not admitting defeat. It is conceding that you are intelligent enough to know when to ask for help.

• Try doing something for someone else. This enables you to get your mind off yourself, and you obtain an extra benefit, in that it strengthens friendships. Stress causes people to turn inward and concentrate too much on their own problems.

• Do first things first. Split your tasks into those that are important and those that are unimportant—delegate the unimportant to others. Learn to say no when you're overloaded or when you're asked to do something you don't consider important.

• Plan how you will spend your time. Recognize the time wasters and eliminate them. Pace yourself by scheduling your jobs, allowing time for the unexpected. Do one thing at a time. It is tension-producing to tackle all your tasks at once. Set some of them aside and work only on the most urgent.

• Work off stress—and try to blow off steam—by exercising. A person in poor physical condition is in no shape to handle stress. Exercise revitalizes you, increasing your emotional and physical strength. Even a walk around the office or factory can help.

• Get enough sleep and rest. Lack of either one can lessen your ability to handle stress by making you more irritable. If stress causes you to lose sleep, inform your doctor. Eat regular, well-balanced meals to assure good nutrition and a reserve of energy.

Costs

Supervisors quickly learn that costs are one of the major factors that influence their decisions. But although cost is always a major consideration, if the cost of a project or undertaking is small in relation to other operations or to the company's total resources, even a bad decision relative to it cannot have too much impact. For control purposes, companies usually set definite limits on the amount of money that managers at various levels can spend for new projects without the approval of their superiors. In all cases, large appropriations and expenditures require the approval of top management.

Most of the cost decisions made by first-line managers involve comparing alternative courses of action. Where the differences in costs can be quantified, it is easier to compare the alternatives. When possible, figures should be converted into the common denominator of money. For example, instead of comparing the number of a certain type of item produced with sales stated in dollars, converting the items into their dollar value will make the comparison easier to understand.

Keep in mind when comparing costs that you want to identify the difference between those costs that would be involved if an alternative decision were made and those that will exist even if the alternative were not chosen. Realize, too, that some costs will not bear on the decision—including them in the problem-solving process would be a mistake. An example of such a cost is the money spent on a project that has already incurred various costs. In making a decision on whether or not to spend more money, that which has already been spent should not be considered. Such an expenditure is a "sunk" cost. The decision should be made on the basis of what future costs will be.

Intangible costs can often be projected into future costs, thus making a comparison possible. A case that a supervisor might encounter is the effect of reduction in employee morale as a result of a low wage scale policy a department might adopt—the problem being the possible labor turnover caused by it. Skilled people might be reluctant to work for low pay and might leave the company. If management is willing to take that chance, a supervisor may be able to estimate that the replacement of certain personnel would cost a specific amount and use this figure as a means of measuring the policy's effect.

Often, a first-line manager's decision involves a trade-off. A trade-off occurs when to handle one problem, you give up handling another. Usually, you make a trade-off decision when you have only so much money to spend and not enough to take care of both problems. For example, you may want both a word processor and a duplicating machine for the office, but your budget will permit you to purchase only one of the two. This is a trade-off situation, in which you must decide which item is more important to your department.

Over the years, many techniques have been developed to assist management, including supervisors, in making decisions involving costs. Many of these are quantitative in nature in addition to being mathematically complex. There is a place for this method of analysis, and first-line managers should be aware of the various procedures used. The subject is discussed in Chapter 6.

Policy

Managers at all levels in a company frequently call upon company policy to guide and aid them in making decisions. Policy is an understanding among members of a group or company that makes the actions of each member in a given set of circumstances more predictable to other members. If a decision provides guidance for other situations, it is said to be a policy decision. Policy decisions thus set precedents for future decisions.

One of the most impersonal elements in any company is its policy. The distribution of policy statements should be limited to those people with an established need to receive them, but all employees should be able to locate any particular policy quickly. A supervisor should have a complete and current set of policy statements directly affecting his or her functions as well as some authority always available to confirm that questionable decisions do not conflict with policy.

Only top management is competent to make true policy decisions. Administrative decisions can be made by department heads and managers, from first-line supervisors up. But the rules regarding where such decisions should be made cannot be exact because decisions made in one department or division of a company may force decisions to be made in others. Also, the distinction between policy decisions and other types of decisions is not always clear in some company situations. Where top management wants to keep close control, it may establish policies that cover much more than general action and thus leave little opportunity for decision making at lower levels in the company.

Management is able to effectively delegate decision making in a company that has strong and clear policies. In most companies, the rules and regulations are actually attempts on the part of executives to exercise authority, to direct subordinates to follow certain courses of action under given circumstances. An example of this control is the authorization levels established for financial expenditures. Under such a system, subordinates can make their own decisions without worrying about whether they have the right to make them.

Although top management usually originates policies to deal with the needs of middle or lower management, policies may also be created in response to subordinates' actions, or to comply with positions taken by trade associations or government agencies. Policies may apply to all departments of a company or only one, yet they are generally considered to be the company's most important decisions. Many organizations require not only that their policies be in writing but that they be collected and assembled in manuals. Such manuals are referred to as standard procedures or standard practice books. Oral policies may also exist, but they risk being overlooked or misinterpreted.

The theory behind the use of manuals is that all the user has to do is figure out which rule applies to the particular problem at hand and then use the position stated in the manual as the sole basis for his or her decision. The range of rules that you can find in policy manuals is usually quite wide, ranging from personnel regulations to product pricing. It is presumed that if you always follow the rules, you will always make good decisions.

Some first-line managers consider a policy manual a great help. They believe that many of their decisions are already made for them if they faithfully use the book. They feel confident that every decision they make on the basis of the directives they find there will be to the benefit of the company in attaining its objectives. Moreover, if they do as the manual directs, they will never get into trouble. Policy manuals enable decision makers who lack self-confidence to make decisions of which they can be sure. Some first-line managers are among those who like policy manuals. They need not take the time and trouble to study a problem if they know it's covered in the book; they can safely delegate those problems to their subordinates.

Since policies play such an important role in decision making, a good policy should be:

- Related to the goals and objectives of the company.
- Written in clear, understandable language.
- Explicit in its limits.
- Flexible to change.
- Reasonable and logical.
- Readily interpretable.

Don't policies have limitations and faults? They certainly do, and some are quite serious. Lack of understanding of a policy is the greatest limitation on its effective use faced by a company and its managerial personnel. A given policy may be unsound in concept or incorrectly stated, thus hindering achievement of company objectives. The climate and environment of business operations may change, calling for a corresponding policy change that is not made; left as it is, the original policy will be misleading and will inhibit effective planning and action. If a supervisor gets in the habit of referring to a company policy as the only basis for his or her action, the supervisor may use it as a crutch and defeat the intent of the policy. Although policies support and provide direction for the actions of managers, if a policy remains in existence long after conditions have changed, it can impede progress. If policies are stated in broad and clear terms, they may tend to encourage managers to avoid taking responsibility for their own decisions.

Rigid adherence to policies often leads to unforeseen and unwanted consequences. People are different, and the situations they get into are seldom exactly alike. However, the person who originated the policy or made the rule had to assume that all the situations covered by that rule in the future would almost exactly duplicate the specific one he or she had in mind when framing it. This is why the rules found in policy manuals often seem unrealistic or impractical to the persons asked to follow them. A supervisor coming across such a rule might be heard to say, "I can see that whoever dreamed this up never worked as a supervisor." In addition, policy regulations usually state (or imply) that the applicable rule is the *only* course of action to be followed by the decision maker. This conflicts with the fact that in order to make good decisions, several alternatives should ordinarily be considered. If a supervisor is required to follow the rule blindly, his or her decision may hurt the company rather than help it.

The less confidence upper management has in the ability of lower management to make good decisions, the more rules it formulates and the more voluminous its policy manuals become. Excessive rules are thought of as "red tape" by those who are hampered by them. It is true that too many rules not only slow down decision making but often result in a loss of respect for the regulations. When a person thinks that the use of a rule will hurt him or her, the person simply bends the rule or discards it and follows his or her own beliefs. However, to protect himself or herself, the person will usually try to make the records look right. If the person and his or her boss both realize that strict adherence to the rule will hurt the company or themselves, chances are they will look for a way out, perhaps seeking a rule that permits them to do as they wish. Or they will collaborate in breaking the rule and falsifying the record. Such rule breaking and falsification frequently occur in companies run mostly by rules and regulations.

If your company policy manual is vague or written in a way that could easily be misinterpreted, the company sooner or later will get in trouble over it. For example, a policy covering unexcused absenteeism may seem perfectly clear in calling for progressive discipline, starting with a written warning for the first offense, then suspension for the second and third, and discharge for the fourth. But if the policy does not clearly define "excused" and "unexcused," first-line managers may have to make the distinction on their own. For some managers, breakdown of one's automobile might be considered a legitimate excuse, while for others, it might be seen as deserving of disciplinary action. In this case, there is a good probability that an arbitrator might reinstate an employee who has been discharged for absenteeism by ruling that the vagueness of the company policy led to inconsistent discipline.

Policy manuals can be of great assistance, with many such drawbacks alleviated or eliminated by stating policies differently. Instead of specific rules, the statements and guidelines should be presented in terms of goals and objectives. They should simply outline the ways and means the users should consider in making their decisions. In this form, a policy manual would be visualized as standard practice instructions designed to ensure consistency and uniformity in handling most standardizable work.

Change

One of the most difficult jobs a first-line manager has to handle is making decisions that call for change. The problem is often one of getting employees to respond positively and constructively to a change instead of opposing it, as so often happens. The most important step in introducing any kind of change is to discuss it with those affected as early as possible. By talking about a change before it's made, you give people time to get used to it. They won't suddenly be surprised by a management decision that may mean they have to work in another area or do their jobs differently than they have been used to. It's only human to oppose such surprises.

If you are planning to make a decision calling for a change in procedure, you can eliminate resentment and gain better acceptance by asking your people for their ideas and letting them help you with the change. Early discussion is also important when changes are originated by upper management. For example, if the company is going to put a computer in your department, it is just about impossible to keep a change like that a secret. As soon as word gets out, the negative aspects of the proposed change are exaggerated, and fear is generated among the employees. Some of them, especially the older ones, become worried about whether they'll be able to operate the computer, while others fear that its introduction will mean they'll lose their jobs. As a result, they plan to fight the change even before it's announced.

A supervisor can prepare his or her people for change by training them and helping them get ready for it. You should train them in planning and goal setting so they become familiar with both of these techniques. Help them to develop skills in setting and achieving objectives. Reward those who do this and withhold rewards from those who do not. As for introducing change and preparing people for it, here are some tips on how to go about it:

• Give only the facts. State only what you *know*, not hope, the company plans to do. Be honest and frank when talking about problems that the proposed change might cause. Explain what it might mean by way of jobs that will be created, altered, or eliminated; retraining that will be required; shifts in work assignments; differences in pay; and other moves you know about. The first words you say about the change are critical because your listeners, being apprehensive, may jump to premature conclusions. If you are unprepared for what to say, you can run into real trouble. Make sure your announcement contains only facts and not opinions. Otherwise, you may be the source of rumors. You could also trigger complaints and grievances.

• Stress the positive features of the impending change. Talk about the things that will benefit everybody, such as a better product, quicker service to customers, and lower costs. Be certain to cover points that pertain directly to your people as well, such as making the work easier, providing a chance to increase their incentive pay, improving safety, and creating better working conditions. Remember that people are more interested in what a change will mean to them personally than in what it will mean to the company.

• Avoid downgrading or bad-mouthing past methods or procedures. In trying to sell something new to your people, you may tend to go overboard in your enthusiasm concerning it. Be careful of what you say about the method of procedure it replaces. If you imply that the old (and present) method is poor and even stupid, the people who used it will resent your saying this because they felt they were doing a good job.

• Recognize that a few adjustments may be necessary. You're bound to run into some reluctance and hesitation whenever people have to change their habits and way of doing things. Expect some grumbling, grousing, and even a lack of cooperation.

Unless the situation deteriorates to the point where quality is affected or work performance measurably drops off, give people a chance to settle down and get used to the new arrangement.

• Follow up. Beware if things seem to be going smoothly the first few days after a change. Some people may be resentful but have kept quiet. Others may be inclined to find fault but have decided to stick with the change a bit longer before voicing their complaints. Others have not accepted it and are simply waiting for its weaknesses and drawbacks to become apparent to you. In this situation, you should follow up to see if your people are having problems that they haven't called to your attention. Give them all the help you can in eliminating the bugs and correcting malfunctions. There will be less resistance to the change when you do so.

Managing change means letting people feel they are in control of their work. You have a great psychological advantage over them if you can bring this off. Most people like to have immediate and frequent feedback on what they are doing. Further, they want to be able to measure their own performance themselves. They need to feel they can correct their mistakes on the spot before things get out of hand and the supervisor has to take over. Any change that provides these benefits will have their support.

Make a complex change in steps, with an assessment period at the end of each. This gives people a chance to understand where they're going, see some benefits early, and get satisfaction from a success. A series of successes will build momentum to proceed at full steam and bring the entire project to completion. Success breeds success. But be aware that there may be a gap between what people say they need and what they can do, given their present aptitudes and skills. You have to close that gap with training and acclimation. Try to compromise between the desire to advance and the ability to adjust to new procedures.

Why People Resist Change

Resistance to change occurs whenever people misunderstand, feel insecure, or fear loss of power or authority. Most people react in one of three ways: socially, by resisting as part of a group; psychologically, by changing their work attitudes; or behaviorally, by changing their work patterns. Change involves the possibility of failure, of having to do things in new, strange, and uncomfortable ways. In the absence of motivation and incentive, it is safer and easier to stay with the status quo.

New machinery is by no means the only kind of change people resist. They may be against any new idea or procedure they think threatens their security—even though the truth is usually just the opposite. Resistance can be expected for many reasons, but the most common are:

- The nature of the change has not been make clear to the people who are going to be influenced by it.
- Those who are going to be influenced by the change did not participate in proposing the change itself.
- Those who are going to be influenced by the change cannot see how they are going to benefit from it.
- People think the change is an indication of their poor performance.
- The change is made on personal rather than impersonal grounds.
- The change requires learning new work habits or new skills.
- The change upsets established social relationships among the workers.

There are other reasons why people resist change; some are based in the subconscious mind and the personality of individuals to such an extent that they are not able to sense them. A few such reasons are: saving face, responding to peer pressure, and opposing leadership in general. People will seldom admit to such motivations, even if they are aware of them.

First-line managers who must combat resistance to change should know the best way to go about it. Offering rewards or bargaining often reduces such resistance. But to use this technique, you must know the actual cause of the resistance. If there seems to be a misunderstanding, face-to-face discussions are good, because questions can be answered directly. Since changes rarely need to be made suddenly, the time allotted to preparing for change should be used to condition people for it. Getting people involved in the change often forestalls resistance to it. Personal involvement reduces fear and misunderstanding. Some companies use trial runs to advantage; the people involved in the change can thereby test a new system before judging it. Trial runs tend to be less of a threat, thus diminishing resistance.

What about the person who openly fights change? Should you clamp down on him or her so others won't follow suit? No. It is likely that this would only focus attention on the dissenter. Your best bet is to listen to what the person is trying to say, bring out his or her hidden concerns, and then try to alleviate them. When you've done that, get the person involved in carrying out the change.

Promoting Acceptance

Introducing a change often becomes complicated because so many people are involved. Not only is a change difficult to introduce and control in a modern office or factory, but if it fails, you may not even be able to tell why. A change will have the best chance of succeeding if you introduce it and promote it in the following manner:

- Change just one thing at a time and make sure the change is measurable so you can gauge its effect.
- Know what to expect from each factor involved. Any deviation will affect the measurement of your change.
- Measure against a control. Two groups of people or machines performing under identical conditions will readily reveal the effect of a change in one.
- Make sure the change is permanent. People may initially respond favorably to a change merely because it breaks the monotony. But when the novelty wears off, they tend to return to their regular methods. Keep track of results for an extended period to be certain your change remains in effect.

We know that people frequently resist change because they wish to remain comfortable and continue with familiar procedures. Yet a company either grows or falls behind depending on how management keeps the organization up to date and competitive. To stay in business, a company must change. People accept change only when they know why it is in their best interests to do so. Being frank in explaining the reasons for a change will accomplish much more toward having it accepted than will niceties, subtleties, partial truths, or outright commands. People are not fooled by insincerity or deceit. They retaliate by simply clamming up and doing things their same old way. An honest explanation, if presented with empathy and candor, can make even distasteful or unpleasant changes tolerable.

When do people welcome change? There are several answers to that question. People welcome change when it means a personal gain for them, real or imagined, in working conditions, pay, status, or authority and when it offers them a new challenge or opportunity. They are also receptive to it when they like and respect the person responsible for it and the way he or she introduces it. And they welcome it when their ideas are considered and the timing is right.

Making Decisions Involving Change

Supervisors need to train and educate themselves to learn and understand change and change techniques, just as they did with planning, scheduling, budgeting, and cost control. They can acquire this knowledge and skill by attending seminars and conferences dealing with interpersonal and intergroup relations, the nature of change, and the importance of cooperation and participation of those who must accept change. Companies that have survived bad times and are growing are those that have learned to handle change effectively. Likewise, successful first-line managers are those who have learned to understand and cope with change.

One of the most significant changes facing organizations is the shift in individual values. Some of the traditional values and ideals seem destined to fade away. Commitment now seems to be more in terms of the task, job, discipline, or profession rather than loyalty to a company. People judge and evaluate jobs on factors other than pay and job content. They consider the type of business or industry, management philosophy in regard to participation, the extent of research and development conducted, and the opportunities for advancement. There is also a strong trend toward placing a higher value on autonomy. Individuals want to have more say in their work and its environment—to control it, not be controlled by it. Acceptance of conditions as they are is being replaced by comparing oneself and one's company to what could be. The usual result is dissatisfaction with the current status.

In order to manage successfully in the age of change, first-line managers should devote their efforts to increasing their mental flexibility—their ability to respond to new problems with new solutions. They should prepare for the future by constantly forcing changes in their habit patterns, such as changing the type of articles and books they read. Their self-improvement programs should include developing skills and abilities in new fields, especially in areas where technology is changing. By cultivating new friendships outside their usual circle, they can broaden their interests in people and what they do. Taking college courses or serving with voluntary civic or political groups will also expand their viewpoints and knowledge. Perhaps the best way for supervisors to prepare and train themselves to make decisions involving change is for them to question how they conduct every phase of their operations; answering the questions of what, where, why, and who related to their jobs will enable them to anticipate change and be ready for it.

To determine how good you are at making decisions involving change, evaluate your past performance in this area. Are your people always more willing to accept a change when you ask for their opinions and ideas before making your decision? If they seriously believe you want their ideas and will consider them, they will be receptive. But if they think you and your boss have already made up your minds, and you are only pretending to consider their advice to make them think they are contributing, they will resent it.

Have you ever announced a change, realized that you'd made a mistake, retracted your decision, and apologized for the mistake? Although pride would keep many supervisors from taking this step, you should have done so. Your people will respect you all the more if you retract a bad decision and admit you were wrong. When your boss made a decision that you felt was a mistake to carry out, did you ask him or her specific questions to learn the reason for the decision? If you did, you handled the situation properly. If the boss didn't convince you, you should have explained to him or her why you thought it was a mistake. Put a feather in your cap if the boss had not considered your point and then modified or reversed the decision.

Companies should consider hiring specialists and professionals to manage major changes. Such firms or groups are classified as "management engineers" and "consultants." They can be brought into the company either part-time or full-time on a contract basis. These people are truly the experts in their areas and invariably perform a valuable function for their clients.

Power and Authority

A number of principles are employed by business and industry in operating and managing an organization. They come into play when assigning employees responsibility and authority. In this sense, they dictate decision making by individual. Some of these principles include rules concerning chain of command, span of control, delegation of authority, and management by exception. First-line managers should be knowledgeable regarding these subjects for several reasons: They should have a complete understanding of the management hierarchy of their company; they should see the relationship between accountability and authority; and they should be aware of how all of these principles affect the decisions they are expected to make.

Chain of Command

The formal organization chart functions properly only if each person knows to whom he or she reports and who reports to him or her. The chain of command is literally a formal statement of who takes orders from whom. Thus, the top person can direct and control the levels of subordinates below, and the first level can direct and control the next lower level. Decision making is treated in the same hierarchical manner. Although the theory behind chain of command is good, it does not always work well as a system for achieving cooperation and permitting individuals to perform at their optimum capability. The problem revolves around the transmission of ideas and the collaboration between lower-level positions in an organization where the individuals are positioned on two different "ladders" of the hierarchy. If the chain-of-command principle were to be strictly followed, communications would have to be made up one ladder and down another. This process would not only be time-consuming but could also result in a final course of action that was inferior to that originally proposed. Another weakness with the chain of command is that there are usually too many levels of supervision or management between the top authority in an organization and the rank and file. If directions flow down from the top through the chain of command and reports on what is actually happening follow the same channel, the longer the chain, the greater the chance that the directions or reports will be distorted along the way.

It is normal for first-line managers to wonder how closely they must adhere to the chain of command in carrying out their responsibilities. By all means, you should conform to the practice in your company. If that is not clear to you, rely on your judgment. Since authority and responsibility are delegated through the channels of a chain of command, it's better to make your decisions through them, too. It avoids doing things without letting your boss know what's going on. Yet there are times when you may want to bypass the system. In emergencies, or when you must make a quick decision, it's logical to get advice or permission from a higher authority other than your boss if he or she is not readily available.

Span of Control

The span-of-control principle attempts to dictate the number of people who should report to an individual. As interpreted by one company, span of control can mean that a supervisor or next-level manager should direct the work of 8 persons—no more and no less—and a vice-president should have 3 or 4 operating divisions under his or her control. But most of today's organizations cannot and do not function under such a rigid rule of thumb. If a work group needs a lot of direction and guidance, then a supervisor needs time to do it. Eight may be the optimum number of subordinates under those circumstances. However, if a work group shows a lot of initiative and is self-regulating, it may function effectively with 10 or even 15 members. Span of control is relative to how the power to control activities is distributed. If a company operates under a system where participative management is practiced in setting goals and supporting one another's efforts, supervision need not be close for the effective coordination of work.

The determination of the optimum number depends on many factors in a given organization and should usually be tied directly to the question of the number of levels in the hierachy. If it appears that a small span of control for each level would work best, then the number of necessary levels will be larger than would be the case with a wider span of control. The organization with many levels will be pictured as tall on its organization chart, whereas the organization with a wide span of control will be seen as flat.

Span of control should focus attention on the basic fact that a supervisor has limitations. First, you have limited time available for your activities. Second, you have limited energy available and must depend on others to help you. And third, the number of subjects to which you can give your attention is limited. These limitations not only support the concept of span of control but also indicate that the optimum span varies among individuals. In addition, the span of control under some conditions will differ from that under other conditions.

Delegation of Authority

As noted earlier, decisions should be made at the lowest competent level in an organization. This means that responsibility and corresponding authority should be delegated as far down in the hierarchy as possible. Some managers believe that responsibility cannot be delegated. Others state that the responsibility of a superior for the acts of a subordinate is absolute. Although it may seem that two contradictory principles are involved, both may be logically accepted. For example, say that Art is a higher-level manager, Betty is his first-line manager, and Carl is Betty's subordinate. Betty can delegate decisions to Carl, but she is still accountable to Art for the results of the decisions. Part of Betty's

71

responsibility is not to delegate decisions to the incompetent, and if her judgment of Carl's competence was in error, she cannot expect Art to excuse her simply because she did not personally make a given mistake.

Although delegation is recognized as a necessary part of managing by most operating executives, in practice it involves risks and costs. Two important factors determine the degree of decentralization desirable in a given situation. First, the skills and competence of subordinates influence the success of any program of delegation. Personnel must be developed who can adequately handle the decisions delegated to them. Second, the distribution of the necessary information and instructions is critical to any delegation. Unless a higher-level manager, supervisor, or subordinate has sufficient information available for a decision, he or she will have little chance of making a good one. Delegation of authority is most successful when it entails collaboration between the superior and the subordinate. By planning together, applying management-by-objectives principles, and agreeing on a course of action, the subordinate carries out the implementation successfully.

As for how much delegating you as a first-line manager should do, delegate when you see that you can't personally keep up with everything you feel you should do. Start by giving routine and minor time-consuming jobs to your people. The trick to delegating effectively is to give minor matters to someone else to handle while spending your own time on the major or more important matters. Be willing, too, to give up certain work that you enjoy. A supervisor must learn to hand out work that subordinates can perform. Otherwise, more significant and more difficult work may not get done. You need not worry about being criticized for delegating to a subordinate work the boss has given to you. Managers should be concerned only with seeing that the job is done the right way, not with who does it.

Management by Exception

Management by exception means that all matters requiring decisions that are routine and for which policies have been established can be handled at any given level in the company by subordinates. But when a problem arises that is not covered by the rules—an exception, so to speak—the subordinate should pass it to higher management for a decision. The exception principle calls attention to the fact that executives at the top levels of an organization have limited time and capacity. They should avoid becoming involved and bogged down with routine matters that can be handled just as well by subordinates. As such, the exception principle is an important concept concerning the delegation of authority in an organization. Attention to the principle can help lower-level managers and supervisors understand exactly what they are expected to do.

First-line managers can apply the exception principle to their work in several ways. They can consider it as a form of delegation in which they permit events to take their normal course so long as they stay within control or prescribed limits. When events get out of line, they can take over and straighten things out. Another way they can use the principle is by setting up systems for handling recurring problems as a matter of routine. What they look for in these cases are the exceptions to the routine. They act only on those matters that are unusual or involve change from standard practice.

Chapter Four

Deterrents and Hindrances— Aids and Simplifications

In making decisions, you will encounter roadblocks, forces that will attempt to dissuade you, interests that stand in your way, and personal inclinations that are not conducive to action on your part. Very likely, the most disturbing of these will be the people who will be affected by your decision if it is not in their interests or to their liking.

Decision makers must frequently contend with conflict and commitment, and they may worry about their credibility. In order to make sound decisions, bias and prejudice cannot be tolerated. But making good decisions is not as difficult and time-consuming as it may appear. Like other disciplines, there are aids and simplifications to make the task easier. You'll find that hunch, common sense, and being able to think quickly will augment your basic skill in the art and enable you to make good decisions most of the time.

Procrastination

Procrastination is simply putting off doing something. It is the biggest roadblock to accomplishment, yet all of us are guilty of it to some degree at one time or another. You procrastinate most often when you are faced with a difficult decision or have an unpleasant job to do. Your position may be even more uncomfortable if you are not convinced that the job really needs to be done at all. For example, your subordinate may finally have learned his or her lesson and may never again need to be disciplined for a certain type of misbehavior.

People procrastinate in various ways. Perhaps you have used one or more of the following "outs" yourself:

- Postponing a job because of "lack of time."
- Substituting a job that is "more important or urgent."
- Getting someone else to do the job.
- Reasoning that "now is not the time for it."
- Being absent at the right time.

Despite the seriousness of procrastinating, you can overcome the problem if you set your mind to it. A good way is to develop a positive, optimistic viewpoint about your job and your duties. Realize that situations usually are not as bad as they may seem. Decide early that you cannot continue to put off something indefinitely.

While getting started on a distasteful job is no easy matter, your best bet is to go after the job when you are fresh and in a good frame of mind. Once you start, keep at it until you finish. This saves facing the unpleasant thing a second time.

An experienced supervisor may actually be doing the best thing when he or she decides to do nothing for the moment, even though it appears, because of his or her experience, that a decision should be made. For example, it has become common practice in some companies today to permit a "cooling off" period to elapse before making judgments on personnel behavioral problems. Better decisions have resulted when there is further investigation before meting out discipline. Emotions are not as likely to be an influence if some time is taken for reasoning.

Procrastination can be a big problem for busy higher-level

managers, supervisors, and those who carry a heavy load of responsibility. While middle- and lower-level managers may allow themselves greater indulgence, the top-echelon people realize that when all the facts are in and there are no strong reasons for delay, they must make a decision. Timidity is not in their vocabularies.

Procrastinating suggests to observers that the person guilty of it has a fear of making decisions or an inability to do so. Successful managers do not hesitate to act and assume responsibility for their judgments. They would not hold their positions otherwise. But not all delay in making decisions should be blamed on procrastination. There is always the danger of swinging too far the other way—making hasty judgments—which can also be bad. A decision maker may refer to a cautious approach to a sensitive situation as "hesitating strategically." The prudent manager may occasionally resort to this explanation when he or she is under pressure and not quite ready to make a move.

A failing of some managers is that they are too willing to ignore a problem. They point out that people who don't make a decision can't be criticized for poor judgment. At least two things are wrong with this thinking. First, taking no action is still looked upon as a decision—that none is necessary. Second, the manager may suffer criticism anyway—that he or she didn't get results because of the failure to act.

Fear or doubt exists in the mind of every person making a major or important decision. The element of risk as well as the magnitude of what may be at stake naturally lead to apprehension. Successful higher-level managers and supervisors may shrug off the suggestion of fear by pointing to the fact that development of specific abilities to cope with problems is the forte of the efficient manager. The person who accepts managerial responsibility should be well organized and adept at problem solving. With his or her confidence and an untiring desire to get things done, the manager should welcome decision making and gain a high degree of satisfaction from it.

Yet even the most calculating, nerves-of-steel individual will occasionally hesitate. The wise manager views decision making with care and respect because he or she recognizes the seriousness and far-reaching consequences of what he or she says and does. Poor decisions can halt a person anywhere on the hierarchy ladder and, if occurring frequently, can cause him or her to drop down a rung or two. The transfer of a first-line manager back to the ranks is an occasional tactic of a company wishing to relieve a poor decision maker of managerial responsibilities.

Practical managers attempt to minimize the "bad decision" syndrome when carrying out their responsibilities. They don't jump recklessly at the first answer to a problem that comes up. They realize, further, that they may not make good decisions if they are under severe stress, emotionally upset, or pressured for quick action. They know that they must "keep their cool" if they are to perform at their best. They may delay making a decision until they feel they are in a better position.

A factor contributing to making a bad decision is the belief that it has to be made right now. Better decisions might be made if the decision maker asked himself or herself, "How much time do I have to make this decision?" and then used all the time available. Procrastination because of caution can be forgiven. A conscious decision not to decide now justifies the decision maker's thinking to hold up until more information can be obtained.

A personnel manager handling union grievances confided to me a few years ago about how he valued his pipe and tobacco at a meeting. When he found himself in a tight situation calling for an immediate decision or for the proper words to forestall one, he gained himself a few valuable seconds to think by filling, tamping, and lighting up his pipe. While this maneuver may have done more to cause irritation among impatient members than it did to calm emotional ones, it still served its purpose to the manager by helping him make acceptable rulings.

As a supervisor, you should practice acting promptly so your boss won't think you are indecisive. Some bosses are inclined to bypass indecisive subordinates and decide for themselves what changes should be made or what should be done. Your boss may do this if you continually stall for time or procrastinate. Also, your people may stop asking you questions if you vacillate and refuse to take a stand on an issue.

Unspecifiable Risk Procrastination

Postponing a decision because of reluctance to take unspecifiable risks sometimes allows a decision maker to await a change that will lead to a more satisfactory solution of a problem. Even recalling rumors, rough analogies, and superstitions can cause concern over risks that are unknown in the sense that they are vague or nonspecific. Much more often, however, there is justification for procrastinating to consider the possibility of risks that the person cannot specify. Whether realistic or not, such concern can serve as a deterrent to impetuous action.

Decision makers differ widely in their thinking about the extent of the information search they should make to check on unknown risks and the criteria they should use to determine that they have enough information to warrant making a final decision. Work patterns, traditions, policies, and publicity as well as the decision makers' emotional reaction to the information uncovered also affect their determination on whether or not to make an intensive study. A common recourse involves repeatedly discussing the pros and cons with many people, including one's subordinates, peers, and superiors. This is not always the most efficient or convenient way to get the facts and information needed, but it does provide opportunities to expand one's knowledge of the situation, and it sometimes alerts the decision maker to risks he or she might not otherwise have thought about.

Fear of Making the Decision

Although every decision maker realizes self-satisfaction from making decisions that turn out well and promote his or her future and that of others, there is a deterrent to the practice—the recognition that those decisions could have been wrong. This thought also leads to concern over *all* the decisions made recently. How many have been right? What percentage have been on the plus side of the ledger? Nobody expects every decision to turn out right, but if recent judgments have been more wrong than right, a person may be inclined to hesitate with the next decision, particularly if it appears to be a questionable one. Fear of damaging outcomes can act as a deterrent to making a decision.

First-line managers occasionally find themselves in situations where they must make a decision that is tough as well as disturbing. For instance, you may feel very uncertain about your position. You may also be concerned that something will come to light that will make you regret a decision you are about to make. Such situations are often painful, but you can be sure of one thing: The more rational your frame of mind, the more likely you are to make the best decision possible under the circumstances.

The first matter to handle when you fear making a decision is to bring your fears into the open where you can contend with them. You may be afraid of what could happen to you, but if you try to imagine the worst, it may not seem too bad, and you can then think with a clear mind. Next, you should try to imagine the best that could happen. Because this approach is encouraging, it also puts you in a better frame of mind. Before long, your fear of making the decision should have diminished, and you should feel better about tackling it.

Accept the fact that no one is always correct and there are few decisions made without disadvantages. No matter which way you go, there are always advantages to going the other way. Recognize that you will make a poor decision now and then. What is of more importance is your overall performance and that you understand that you're not perfect. This realization should push you to better and better decisions as you move ahead in your career.

Another thing you can do when you're afraid to make a decision is talk to someone about it. While you may hesitate to do this because it might look as if you are indecisive, this will not prove to be the case. Besides, most people are willing and even flattered to listen to someone who has a problem (within limits, of course). Whether or not their comments or advice prove of value, you will have had the opportunity to "unload" your troubles and consequently will feel better about them.

Fear of a Rub

From experience, most decision makers realize that in addition to the known uncertainties about the outcome of a decision, there may be hidden drawbacks. Even the best plans may be imperfect because of a "catch" or "rub." The fear of a rub most commonly arises when you face a decision that is traditionally considered "chancy."

When decision makers have little or no pressure on them to make an immediate decision, their fears of a rub cause them to postpone committing themselves after they have already selected what they consider the best alternative. Often, however, such a delay is brief. Most people limit themselves to a quick search and assessment. If nothing seems out of line, they proceed. But if something comes up to suggest a hidden risk or rub, they may delay their decision for a long time, long enough for them to conduct an entire new study.

People under strong pressure to make up their mind—great enough that they could not postpone the decision without suffering a loss—will continue to worry about the unknown risks they might have let themselves in for even after they have committed themselves. In such a frame of mind, they may show signs of regretting their choice.

When a reluctant decision maker seemingly can't make up his or her mind, an observer may be inclined to say, "What is he (or she) waiting for? Doesn't he (or she) realize that anything anyone ever does in life has some unknown risk?" Compulsive people regularly bring on this kind of reaction because they continue to have doubts about the unknown risks present in every decision, whether it is a matter of choosing a career path or choosing a place to eat lunch. But they are certainly not the only ones who fear unknown consequences and therefore procrastinate.

Worry That a Decision Might Be Regretted

Undoubtedly, there are wide individual differences relating to personality and style in the capacity to tolerate stress in making decisions. If you are reflective as well as apprehensive, you will characteristically approach problems with caution and will almost always be inclined to think about and look for potential losses. Such people move slowly in making decisions and attempt to postpone them as long as possible, even with relatively unimportant matters. At the other extreme are people who can't tolerate uncertainty, delay, and frustration. They are often impulsive and will commit themselves without carefully looking for information and asking for advice.

Every first-line manager undergoes embarrassing and sometimes painful experiences as a result of decisions that have turned out badly. They thus receive lifelong training in the consequences of making too hasty a decision. Accordingly, many managers are likely to be reluctant to commit themselves to a new course of action, such as discontinuing a long-standing procedure in the office or factory, without first obtaining relevant information and thinking over the desirable and undesirable outcomes that might result. Having learned from the disruption, even chaos, that ensued from impulsive decisions in the past, most of them become vigilant when they have to make a decision in the face of uncertainties that could affect their future welfare.

Anticipatory regret is an appropriate expression for referring to the psychological effects of the various worries that beset a decision maker before any losses actually occur. It includes concerns about each of the four major types of undesirable consequences that ensue from making decisions: losses for self, losses for others, self-disapproval, and social disapproval. Such worries, including feelings of guilt and shame, bring about doubt and hesitation and cause the decision maker to realize that even the most attractive of available alternatives might turn out badly. Worry that a decision will be regretted has the value of motivating the decision maker to carefully weigh all the factors. One of its tenets is to delay gratification. The decision maker tolerates the stress of worry and doubt in order to gain the benefit of a better decision in the future. In other words, decision makers must put up with stress during the steps of making a decision if they are to be realistic rather than influenced by wishful thinking.

Even though anticipatory regret may sometimes lead to excessive procrastination, it often results in better decisions. Worrying about what might happen motivates the decision maker to look for reliable and dependable information and to seek expert advice during the decision-making period, even after a tentative choice has already been adopted.

Stimulants of Worry

What circumstances bring on worry? Although many and varied conditions and situations may initiate worry, five are more frequently experienced than others. They are:

- The possibility that new information concerning a decision will come to light.

- The likelihood that the preferred choice is not necessarily superior to another alternative.
- The probability that negative consequences of the decision will materialize almost immediately after the decision is made.
- The fact that influential persons in the decision maker's world view the decision as important and will expect the decision maker to adhere to it.
- The fact that influential persons in the decision maker's world are not pushing for the decision and instead are expecting the decision maker to delay taking action until all the alternatives are carefully evaluated.

These five worries deserve discussion in more detail in order to clarify one's concern that a decision might be regretted.

If a decision maker is led to believe that no new information concerning a decision is likely to come to light, he or she will stop looking for it and seek some other way to reduce the stress of decision making. With this knowledge, higher-level managers and supervisors may deliberately withhold vital information so as to influence a decision in their favor. They may fail to mention the drawbacks to a proposal they wish to sound good, or they may give unwarranted assurances that persuade employees, clients, or customers to be unconcerned about personal values that might conflict with the company's interests. For example, in making an offer to promote an individual to a supervisory position, a higher-level manager may play up the pay, good working conditions, fringe benefits, opportunity for advancement, and high prestige of the job but be careful not to say anything about its disagreeable or unpleasant aspects. Managers of industrial and commercial organizations may attempt to influence employees' decisions in such a way that they will make choices favorable to the organization's interests rather than their own without being completely aware of it.

When you study all the alternatives and conclude that you have only one course to follow, you are likely to ignore the risks inherent in this course and spend little time thinking about the possibility of subsequent loss. If you have no information about obvious drawbacks, you will tend to take action promptly. If all but one alternative seems too dangerous or too costly to consider, decision makers see themselves as having essentially no choice. The illusion of having no real choice or a very limited range of choices gets around indecision. It allows decision makers to stop worrying and passively make the decision since there seems to be nothing else they can do. Of course, the perception that one has no real choice is unfortunately not always an illusion. In some companies, autocratic managers make most if not all decisions of any consequence for their subordinates. Such policies may have long-term detrimental effects, not only on the subordinates' decision-making capabilities but also on their morale and ambition. Instances of illusory lack of choice may occur when people consult with or seek the advice of other professionals. The more respected the adviser and the more vividly he or she pictures the losses that will occur unless his or her advice is followed, the more likely it is that the decision maker will have the illusion of no choice.

Although a decision maker may be aware of a possible loss that could cause future regret, he or she will tend to consider that loss trivial instead of trying to find out how serious it might be if he or she believes that it will not happen soon. Many young first-line managers holding jobs in nuclear or chemical industries know that they could develop cancer because of exposure to radiation or pollutants. Yet they feel relieved when they learn that the danger is unlikely to materialize in less than 20 years' time. By postponing the danger to the distant future, they avoid the stress of making current decisions relating to exposure. The remoteness of negative consequences is demonstrated not to be cause for concern in situations in which decision makers are told that their decisions will not be implemented until other persons perform a series of potentially time-consuming steps. If you know that a questionable decision you make today will not be put into practice for at least two years, you will not be overly worried that your decision might be regretted.

When others view your decision as important, it's natural for you to make sure it will not be regretted. On the other hand, you are inclined not to worry that a decision might be regretted when it appears that the decision is of minimum importance or can be reversed easily. Any indications that a decision can be kept secret, that there are few if any who will be interested in finding out about it, or that the cost of reversal is minimal or nil encourages a decision maker to be relatively unconcerned about potentially negative consequences. In a similar vein, when a decision maker is led to believe that no one will care whether or not he or she subsequently reverses the decision, there will be less care or concern that the decision might be regretted.

A condition that causes a decision maker to become very anxious to end the stress of deciding is pressure from others, especially if they are influential, to make the decision quickly. In business and administrative decision making, pressures come from superiors and peers within the company who are waiting for the decision in order to carry out their own responsibilities or in order to make their own decisions coincide with it. Under such conditions and in such situations, decision makers worry little that a decision will be regretted. In the case of a job offer, for example, some authorities in business and industry can become quite adept at sending out the message that "If you don't accept the job today, it will no longer be available to you." This type of pressure fosters excess vigilance among employees who are already under stress. When this threat is combined with the implied thought that anyone who delays accepting the job in order to get more information about it is unenthusiastic, overcautious, or even disloyal and therefore no longer worthy of the offer, it is doubly lethal.

Rationalization

Rationalization often occurs under the guise of making good decisions. Instead, it is really a misrepresentation. People who rationalize attempt to justify what they have done despite facts that might conceivably have led them to a different decision. We believe that we look at the alternative courses of action open to us, evaluate them, and come to a conclusion. In reality, however, the conclusion frequently precedes the premises. When we have a problem, we quickly reach a conclusion, then go back and try to find reasons to support that conclusion.

Another form of rationalization is the interpretation of facts, either deliberately or unconsciously, to support preconceived ideas. You rationalize "early" when you search for facts that will support the decision you intend to make.

Even if you feel that you reached a decision without rationalizing, it's a good idea to think a bit more about how you arrived at it. Ask yourself if you consciously or otherwise avoided taking into consideration any information that had a bearing on the decision. Review whether your decision was suspiciously close to what you personally would like to do and whether you tended to consider only those facts that reinforced your personal inclinations. If you can honestly answer those questions with an unequivocal no, you can say that you haven't rationalized.

First-line managers may not always be aware that they are guilty of rationalization. Preferably, they want their decision making to be free of this method of reaching and justifying their judgments.

Conflict

It is generally believed that conflict is a major deterrent to making decisions. Some managers feel that communication failures that cause misunderstandings are the principal causes of conflict. They add that others are personality clashes, value and goal differences, poor performance, differences over the way to do a job, issues of who is responsible for what, and lack of cooperation.

Yet hostility and controversy can be a positive and creative force that enables us to grow as employees and help our company to be profitable and remain competitive. Unresolved conflict diverts attention from the job. Employees may form groups to confront their supervisor or higher levels of management with their differences of opinion. Cooperation may drop off while suspicion and distrust are expressed. An attitude of indifference may prevail. By resolving conflict, you can clear the air, increase employee involvement, and promote creative communication and problem solving.

Supervisors differ in the way they attempt to handle conflict. Those who try to force their viewpoint at the expense of others without regard for their preferences set up a win-lose situation in which someone will suffer, resulting in more conflict instead of less. Supervisors who lean toward compromising as an answer look for solutions that provide some degree of satisfaction to the conflicting parties. They may also try to smooth matters over by emphasizing areas of agreement and deemphasizing areas of difference.

The managers who withdraw from a conflict demonstrate their attitude by being quick to comply or conform. They usually remain neutral when there's a need to take a stand. Since resolving conflict requires empathy and equality but not neutrality, their position is untenable because by its nature it settles nothing. Fear is the basis of the withdrawer's approach to conflict.

So how should you handle conflict in the office or factory? Your best solution to the problem is to take the attitude that you're going to do something about it regardless of the consequences. Collect the facts to support your position, document your points, and act.

Loyalty

The goals first-line managers adopt to take care of their personal needs are primarily self-centered. But that doesn't mean that they won't also try very hard to further the goals of the people and the organizations to which they are loyal. Managers who are loyal to the goals and standards of the profession in which they have been trained, or to the goals of their church or community, will sometimes pause to visualize the impact of their decisions on the goals of those organizations. In addition to these loyalties, managers are usually strongly loyal to the department and the company for which they work.

Unfortunately, not all employees are loyal to their companies. People demonstrate their lack of loyalty in different ways, both on and off the job. Most of the time they are unaware that their actions hurt the company as well as themselves. Supervisors should be on the alert for disloyalty and should act when they see or hear indications of it. What should supervisors do? Here are a few examples of employee disloyalty along with the proper course of action the employees and you should follow:

• When employees take advantage of their companies by doing the bare minimum of work in addition to saying that they are not concerned about the welfare of the company, they should be talked to about their attitude and told they need to change their thinking. Their value on the job depends not only on their talents and abilities but also on their willingness to use their skills in ways that are most helpful to the company. Tell them that you are going to observe how they act in the future, and if you don't see an improvement, you will decide what disciplinary action to take.

• Employees who are under stress sometimes make promises that they later decide not to keep. This is particularly true when they realize there is no company rule holding them to their word. For example, a promise to notify you in advance of being absent can be a serious matter when a schedule must be met or when a replacement must be provided to keep up the flow of work through the office. Although you may appeal to the employees' loyalty and to their conscience to keep their word, you may only get more promises. Nevertheless, give people like this several chances before you take disciplinary action. If the matter turns out to be one of morals only and the person continues to fail to keep his or her promises, you may as well start looking for other ways to handle the situation, such as training a replacement for the person. You'll never solve the problem if you don't.

• When an employee criticizes the company in public and downgrades it at every opportunity, he or she is showing extreme disloyalty. Employees should be concerned about their company's problems, profitability, and future. Loyal employees can make a company, and disloyal ones can break it, especially when the company provides services to the public. If you learn that an employee is complaining about the company outside the office or factory, caution him or her about the practice. Explain why such behavior is dangerous and demeaning, not only to the company but also to the person complaining. Ask the disgruntled employee to come to you with any and all complaints. You will decide what can be done about them.

Commitment

The quality of deliberation on a problem that takes place before a decision is made is greatly influenced by the decision maker's thought that he or she will be bound to the decision. Several factors tie people to their decisions and impel them to follow a course despite adverse comments and criticism. Decisional stress depends partly upon the extent to which a decision maker feels committed to adhere to a course of action upon receiving warnings or encountering roadblocks that motivate him or her to change. The more committed the person is to the course of action, the greater the stress generated whenever there is a temptation to change. The decision maker knows that failure to stay on the chosen course may lead to penalties, adverse criticism, and loss of prestige. Anticipation of these various types of losses provides a threat that operates as a deterrent to making a change in course.

Whenever a decision is supported by documentation or a formal legal contract, the cost of changing one's mind is another reason for sticking to the decision. The firmer and more binding a contract and the more drastic the penalties or punishment for breaching it, the stronger the incentive to avoid change. Failure to honor a contract can tarnish one's reputation as well as result in social disapproval.

Social and Personal Constraints

One of the most pervasive constraints or restrictions on changing a decision is the real or political pressure that prevails whenever other people in the decision maker's world know about his or her decision. Often after making a commitment, the decision maker suddenly realizes that others are affected by the decision and expect him or her to hold to it. Being branded as unstable or inconsistent is in itself enough to dissuade one from even discussing with others the possibility of reversing a decision. The greater the number of those in the decision maker's world who are aware of a decision, the more powerful the incentive to avoid the social disapproval that might result from reversal.

If you put a lot of time and energy into a project, you tend to believe that you are doing the right thing and it will work out according to your plan. Similarly, after arriving at a decision that has required a great deal of study and emotional effort, a person is reluctant to admit that the decision has a serious flaw and that all the hard work was futile and should be scrapped. In addition, when you are tired or emotionally drained, you are in no mood to rethink a decision or reactivate an issue that you had just settled.

It is not merely a matter of being lazy, or of not wanting to work again on the same problem, or even of being bored due to over-familiarity with all the alternatives. All of these factors may be involved, but a new type of mental inertia arises after you have announced a decision. It is the threat of self-disapproval for violating your image as an effective, reliable person who is decisive and keeps his or her word. Your esteem and ego are likely to be involved once you say you have made your decision; you don't intend to think about it anymore. To avoid seeing yourself as vacillating, weak-minded, or undependable, you reject any suggestion that you reconsider your decision. You stick to your guns, even after you have started to suspect that you made a bad choice.

Personal constraints brought on by the threat of violating your image, whether you defend one of your earlier stands or a new one, provide a strong dedication to carrying out a plan. People sometimes make use of these constraints to fight their personal weaknesses in following through on a difficult course of action such as giving up smoking or gambling. People who want to give up smoking but do not trust themselves may announce their intention and even make a bet that they will not smoke, so that later they will not be free to change their mind. How-to and self-help booklets often recommend this approach to strengthen your resolve. The texts point out that when you are seriously tempted to smoke, the thought of all the kidding and laughter you'll get for giving in may enable you to get past the crisis. The image of oneself being embarrassed or humiliated probably helps to prevent backsliding because it poses the threat of self-disapproval as well as social disapproval.

Degree of Commitment and Entrapment

Of course, commitment is not an all-or-nothing proposition. The degree of commitment is a function of social and personal constraints, each of which motivates a person to stick to the decision because of new incentives resulting from announcing the decision. The higher the degree of commitment, the greater the cost of reversing the decision and the greater the resistance to regretting it because of any challenging event or incident. But what happens when a decision maker receives negative reactions that might make him or her regret the decision? There are several ways in which a high degree of commitment acts as a deterrent to changing to a new course of action.

The higher the degree of commitment to a prior choice, the less likely that a challenged decision maker will lightly dismiss the risks of changing to another alternative. The higher the degree of commitment, the higher the probability that when alternatives are being considered, the challenged decision maker will be pessimistic about finding a course of action better than the current one. And finally, the higher the degree of commitment, the higher the probability that if a different course of action is temporarily selected as the best one, it will nevertheless be rejected as inadequate when a binding decision is made.

In the course of making a decision, the more binding and consequential a decision is expected to be, the more vigilant and watchful the decision maker will become in trying to make a choice. He or she must look ahead to foresee what additional requirements and involvements might be entailed in the decision. Even the most vigilant decision maker occasionally becomes trapped in a series of decisional obligations never imagined, let alone planned, when the commitment was made. If you are not cautious, you can be very vulnerable to such traps.

Although commitment entrapment may often be attributed to simple carelessness on the part of the decision maker, it also results from clever manipulators or schemers who raise their demands once a person has made an innocent commitment. There is also a third type of trap, typified by the hidden "package deal," which may include both types. A package deal means a series of small commitments that are difficult to turn down once the first commitment has been made. It is hidden in the sense that if the person were aware of what was going on and what was expected to happen, he or she would be inhibited from making the first, seemingly easy, commitment. A first-line manager may readily agree, for example, to donate some time or sign a petition to back a good community cause. The manager may discover afterward that other people involved in that cause expect him or her not only to do the same kind of thing again but to do much more and will be unhappy if he or she fails to do so. As a result, the manager worries about loss of prestige and about being embarrassed by failing to take what others regard as the expected next steps. Once trapped in such a commitment game, the manager may try to preserve his or her reputation by rationalizing that he or she knew all along what was happening and that there is now a realization that he or she wants to buy the entire package.

Commitments are sometimes made gradually over a short period of time until the nonwary decision maker finds himself or herself trapped into a binding unwanted decision. On such occasions, the decision maker suddenly realizes that "now it's too late to get out of it." Entrapment may involve a series of acts, ending in a crime that a person would ordinarily refuse to commit. A psychological reversal to the stepwise escalation sequence is the technique used by astute arbitrators to arrive at a compromise. Such tactics are often referred to as "fractionating" a large problem into a group of smaller, minimally acceptable decisions that everyone will accept.

The making of a small request to pave the way for getting a person to later accede to a large request is commonly known as getting your foot in the door. The technique is used by manipulative people to trap the unwary. It involves an escalating commitment sequence that is similar to the hidden package deal. The technique, practiced most widely by salespersons, relies on the assumption that once the prospective customer has been talked into opening the door and letting the salesperson show his or her samples, the prospect is set up to buy whatever the salesperson has to offer.

There are four explanations for why the foot-in-the-door technique is effective. The first involves the idea that once a person agrees to start doing something, he or she finds it difficult to offer a good excuse for not continuing to do much the same thing. Because of the precedent set, he or she is in no position to appeal to principles as an excuse for taking exception. A second explanation involves a social factor. Once having agreed to an initial request, a person may believe that the other party has been led to expect him or her to go along with a second request. The person doesn't want to disappoint the requester, which might bring on disapproval, and so feels obligated. The third explanation deals with being involved. Once having done something, no matter how minor, about an issue, the person becomes more concerned with the problem. More thought is put into it; accordingly, he or she is more likely to decide to take further action if asked. The last explanation concerns the change in the person's feelings about getting involved in action. Once someone has agreed to a request, the person becomes, in his or her own eyes, one who agrees to requests made by strangers, who takes action on things believed in, and who cooperates with good causes.

Commitment Warnings

If decision makers learn that they will be expected to stick to whichever courses they choose, they are likely to become worried about what they might be letting themselves in for. Such commitment warnings deter them from rationalizing that there is no harm in trying out a given choice; they can always try another if this one doesn't work. Similarly, if there is no deadline pressure, becoming worried over the consequences of commitment tends to make a person careful. Therefore, it also makes for more conscientious search and study. The tendency to evaluate alternatives in a biased rather than an objective way is diminished by warnings that the choice will be binding.

Suppose a supervisor is asked by his or her management to choose a lathe that the company is going to purchase for the engineering shop. Each of two models has its own distinctive advantages. These advantages affect the engineering department's expectations of how easy the lathe will be to operate and how accurate and maintenance-free the lathe will turn out to be. Now, let us say the supervisor is told by both lathe manufacturers that the company can get its money back "if not fully satisfied" after trying out the lathe in the company shop. With this new information, the supervisor is likely to arrive at a decision much more rapidly, because he or she would have little realistic hope of finding a machine better than his or her first choice. There is also the knowledge that if the lathe turns out to be unsatisfactory, the decision can easily be corrected at very little cost—the small amount of time and effort required to return the lathe. In contrast, if the supervisor were informed that his or her choice will be final and binding, he or she would be more worried about regretting the decision and would tend to study the alternatives more carefully.

Getting Facts

You need facts when seeking information to enable you to make a decision. The problem is that you must be as sure as you can possibly be that what you call facts are truly that and not merely hearsay. You must also realize that all facts are capable of or susceptible to change. What was true yesterday may not be true today or tomorrow. When few or no facts are available, you must fall back on the information at hand. The problem here is that opinion may be well mixed in with the information. This isn't necessarily bad if the information sources are reliable and if the opinions are authoritative. In addition, when accumulating data, you must recognize and avoid some traps.

Misdirection is one of those traps. Misdirection is getting the right answer to the wrong question. You probably won't have any trouble in getting the right answer because there are lots of people around who are willing to give it to you, provided you ask the right question. People are most easily misdirected when they try to get answers without asking the questions directly. Another way you can experience misdirection is by talking to someone who you consider an expert but who basically isn't (at least on your problem). What happens in this case is that the person doesn't know the answer to your question, but rather than admit it, he or she shifts the question from the one you asked to one he or she can answer. This can be done so cleverly that you believe your question has been answered.

Explanation and meaning are requisites for understanding data and information. The same group of facts can be interpreted in more than one way. Avoid blind faith in an expert. Instead, determine whether, given the expert's data, you would have arrived at the same conclusions. Such a step is wise because if something just doesn't seem right, you can ask the expert to explain it. The most dangerous explanation is one that distorts the facts. The person who provides the information has an obligation to present it in such a manner that you will understand it the same way he or she does. For example, if waste in the factory has gone up from 5 percent to 10 percent, should one say it has gone up 5 percent or 100 percent? Both answers are correct, although in different senses. The pessimist may use one and the optimist the other. A realist avoids the percentage figure entirely and says that waste has doubled—a statement that cannot possibly be misunderstood.

Connotation is the suggesting of a word's meaning apart from the thing it explicitly names or describes. While it is natural to try to get all the meaning out of a statement or remark, you may sometimes get more than was intended by the speaker or writer. For example, if your boss says to you after hearing about a decision you intend to make, "If it doesn't work out as you expect, we'll have to make some changes," how do you take that remark? If you are a secure person, you take it to mean that you should change your approach to the problem. But if you are an insecure person, you might take it to mean that your job is in jeopardy.

Another term that decision makers need to treat with care and attention is *average.* The word *average* has several meanings when applied to particular data. If the number of instances or incidents involved is large enough, minor differences will be negligible, since all the methods of calculating the average are then likely to result in values that are very close. But if the number of instances is small, the arithmetical average (a quotient) may be far from the mean or median (the value in the middle) or mode (that which occurs most frequently). Averages, of course, cover up extremes, and that is why decision makers like to use them when dealing with units and figures. If you want to check the validity of an average, do the following: Determine whether more than 50 percent of the instances deviate from the average by more than 25 percent or whether more than 25 percent of the instances deviate from the average by more than 50 percent. If either of these determinations proves to be the case, the validity of the average should be questioned.

When to Stop Seeking Facts

In getting information and data to help you make a decision, be aware that there is a limit to how far you should go. Probably you will never have all the facts in making some decisions. But you would like as many as possible to increase your chances of doing the right thing. The time to stop seeking information and make the decision is when additional input duplicates previous information and when additional facts are trivial.

Experienced managers also say that you should bring your information search to an end when the cost of obtaining more information exceeds its worth. They add that the more critical and lasting the effect of a decision, the more you can afford to go after the last bit of data. You shouldn't, for example, spend a lot of time (and money) on a temporary procedure you're adopting in your process or service if within a short period of time you will be installing a new permanent procedure.

However, never use the lack of information as an excuse for procrastinating. When you are faced with a decision that is difficult to make or unpleasant to carry out, put off the temptation to delay it by asking for more information. A person who may be pressuring you for a decision will not be fooled by this ploy, and seldom does the additional information make your decision any better.

Be careful about how quickly you make decisions that involve people. Someone may attempt to push you for a quick decision on a certain matter, implying, for example, that unless you act immediately, something drastic or fearful may happen. If you sense that the urgency is forced, it will often pay you to wait a bit. The situation may soften or change considerably, or the person may feel quite differently about the matter within a short time.

Bias and Prejudice

A biased person is inclined to display a highly personal and unreasoned distortion of judgment. When you are prejudiced, you have an opinion or leaning adverse to something without just grounds or before sufficient knowledge is obtained. Obviously, both characteristics are detrimental to the making of good decisions. Thus, when you are seeking information, you should try to get it from people who are neither biased nor prejudiced. However, if you have no other source of information than a biased one, you simply have to estimate the degree of bias present.

Practically every reply to a question will have some bias behind it, if for no other reason than that most people prefer to be agreeable rather than disagreeable and also want to appear knowledgeable. An unbiased or straight answer is seldom expected from a leading question or from one that is ambiguous.

Because people have definite social, moral, and political views, the presence of bias must always be considered likely. Yet it is often sufficient to know that bias exists so that you can make the proper evaluation. Always be suspicious of unasked-for claims of being unbiased. For example, when you hear, "Some of my best friends belong to the union," don't be sure that the speaker doesn't dislike unions.

Biased people are prone to repeat their mistakes because they feel the same way about a situation or problem time after time. Take, for instance, the individual who feels that a minority person can't be trusted when promises are made. There are honest and capable people of all races and religions. You are bound to be wrong most of the time if you never deal with a minority. Being biased will prevent you from taking advantage of opportunities to improve yourself. Being prejudiced will deny you the friendship and cooperation you need from others to succeed on the job.

Perhaps the worst thing about being biased or prejudiced is the difficulty you have in changing your thinking so that you don't continue through your career with such a viewpoint. You can overcome this problem by looking for the good in people and the pluses in bad situations. You will find that you will make fewer bad decisions and seldom, if ever, repeat one. Include other people in working out your problems on the job. You will accomplish more and have more friends with whom to share your successes.

Bias About Safety Issues

Since most first-line managers are involved with safety to at least some degree in their activities on the job, it is appropriate to examine some commonly held biases about safety issues that affect decision making. Safety biases, it seems, show up everywhere: in the carrying out of business procedures, in the personal feelings of personnel holding safety jobs, and in the feelings of management toward the discipline.

Because they don't understand how safety can contribute to better management, many upper-level managers tend to prefer shop and factory experience rather than decision-making expertise when selecting safety personnel. To these administrators, safety is a mechanical function based mostly on common sense, heavily loaded with rules and regulations. This bias explains top management's tendency to select persons for safety jobs who are experienced in working with things rather than those who have shown skill in working with people.

With respect to safety activities, here are a few managerial biases that might be questioned for their validity:

• Safety goals and objectives are employee-oriented and not consistent with the goals of the company, such as to make a profit.

• Safety people are the purveyors of doom and destruction in addition to being do-gooders who are heedless of cost.

• Whenever there is a safety infraction, it is probably the supervisor's fault.

• Safety people can't handle themselves before intellectual groups. They are unable to reason, they take too long to make a point, and their reports are poorly organized.

On the other hand, safety people also have biases. Here are a few examples of what some safety personnel believe management thinks about safety:

• Managers seldom take accident statistics seriously when making decisions. Safety rates low in comparison to the other factors involved in running a business.

• The company feels little remorse over bad accident records. Management decision makers are not concerned with safety in the office or factory.

• Safety personnel generally report to a manager whose major responsibilities lie in other areas.

• Safety people do not participate in top-level decision making even when safety is a part of the planning function.

• Safety is not a full-time job; therefore, safety personnel usually have other responsibilities in addition to those concerning safety.

Obviously, some of these statements are far from the truth. Yet they are frequently heard in some companies. Publicly, all companies promote and support safety. But within the company offices, the expense, time, and trouble of conducting a safety program often make the effort a chore to those involved.

Employees can sense when supervisors are not wholehearted in their commitment to safety policy. For example, an employee who hates wearing safety goggles won't change his or her opinion on the matter just because he or she is promoted to a supervisory position. As a supervisor, the individual must now demand that others wear safety goggles because the company policy dictates it. This puts the supervisor in a biased position. Adherence to the rule is given lip service; employees are quick to see that the supervisor doesn't really go along with the rule.

Another area where bias is very evident is in filling out accident reports. Few people like to have it known that they made a mistake, because the implication is strong that someone may not have made the proper decision. Bias is apparent, and face saving interferes with responsibility to the point where the accident report contains pat answers that are of little value in preventing future accidents. Safety inspections by government agencies are seldom welcomed by industry because of the fear of loss of trade secrets. Small companies have a biased concern that they should not be included in state and federal safety checks—that firms with fewer than 25 employess should be excluded. Give us time to prepare for a safety inspection, say many administrators.

Safety professionals must recognize the role they play in business and industry—that is, to warn, advise, and recommend. Many biases can be eliminated if they play that role and no other.

Heuristic Reasoning

We sometimes get involved in heuristic thinking in our attempts to solve a problem. Heuristic means "serving to discover." A definition of heuristic is: of or relating to exploratory techniques (such as the evaluation of feedback) to improve performance.

Heuristic reasoning is reasoning that is plausible yet lacking in strict and precise proof. The method for obtaining the proof has yet to be discovered. Many times in reasoning and inferring, we can proceed only with a faith that when the whole scheme is clear, the proof will follow. With some problems, however, the only way we can make any progress at all is to have the courage to tackle the unknown without any assurance that we will be successful; there are elements of uncertainty in almost any kind of innovation, discovery, and invention. After we succeed and are certain of our course, we can consolidate and make our position look sure and secure.

The heuristic approach is to find out what problems have to be solved even if we cannot come up with a good technique for solving them. The key to discovery is to keep your goals in mind, focus on the unknown, and understand the process of solving problems. Confusion between heuristic thinking and rigorous proof has at times downgraded heuristics. Heuristic thinking is tentative and plausible, but usually not supported by proof. When a problem solver presents a heuristic argument as rigorous proof, critics may question whether he or she appreciates the standards of strict proof.

Heuristic thinking is still in the realm of art. Ways in which the human mind and the machine retrieve information in the process of probing and discovering are being studied. Experimenters are trying to find ways to arrive at discoveries and judgments with less search effort—that is, through concentrating especially on retrieving information and narrowing alternatives for further search. The hope is that discovery and judgment can progress further down the path that has a degree of mystery, intrigue, and art at one end and a degree of system, order, and science at the other.

Intuition and Hunch

Most of today's technical professionals, psychologists, and consultants agree that the creative hunch or intuition is one of the most dramatic as well as useful ways of solving a problem. If your hunches haven't turned out well, perhaps they were not really hunches at all but only wishful thinking or an emotional reaction brought on by prejudice or bias.

What is a hunch? How is intuition defined? A hunch is reasoning that is done unconsciously. A person with a hunch can often come up with a way to solve a problem beyond what normal thought would probably lead to. Intuition is defined as a case of the mind rapidly performing the steps of induction and deduction in analytical thought below the level of conscious awareness.

Intuitive thinking differs greatly from analytical thinking in that it doesn't proceed in careful steps, one at a time. It involves perception of the entire problem and leads to jumping about, skipping steps, and taking the shortest, quickest route to the answer. Analytical thinking follows careful and deductive reasoning, often with a process of induction and experiment and frequently using mathematics, logic, or statistical analysis. The analytical thinker can report the steps leading to the conclusion. The intuitive thinker has an answer that may be right or wrong, but there is no awareness of how the answer was reached.

Although many decision makers do not realize it, intuition or hunch is the basis for quite a few of their decisions. But what is sometimes labeled as intuition is actually a decision based on emotion or knowledge that is not always recalled at the moment. Your brain picks up and stores information without your being aware of it.

You may make a personal decision based almost entirely on intuition without justifying it, but you can't get away with this in government or business. Imagine, for example, the board of directors of a large company announcing they have intuitively decided to build a new plant. Stockholders would certainly demand that they justify their decision. Although you may make a decision now and then based on intuition, you are usually better off having supporting facts for it. The decision will be easier to live with.

You may wonder if a decision based on intuition and hunch is as good as one based on logic. It at least partly depends on how perceptive, observant, cognizant, and knowledgeable of human nature the decision maker is. There is no denying that many decisions based on hunch have proved to be correct. But it is true, too, that they are harder to defend when they turn out to be bad. The use of logic in reaching a decision is not subject to liking, disliking, and irrelevancy. It is also more explainable. The most successful decision makers believe that their best decisions have evolved from a combination of both logic and hunch.

Some supervisors are better than others at intuitive thinking. If you feel that you are quite good at this but are not entirely sure of yourself, here are some suggestions to consider and act on:

• Determine, first, whether you really have intuitive ability. Make a record of your hunches and grade them on how good they were. If the majority have worked out well, give more weight to your future hunches.

• Recognize that you still need basic facts and information

before you can rely on your hunches. Intuitive thinking is a normal thinking process. It has nothing to do with mystical ceremonies or clairvoyance. You must thoroughly investigate every problem.

• Watch for bias and prejudice from personal, subjective thinking. Don't confuse intuitive thinking with wishful, emotional thinking.

• Prefer to use intuitive thinking and analytical thinking together. Depending on the problem, one or the other should predominate. It is not necessary that you give them equal weight in coming to your final decision.

Common Sense

Common sense backs up decisions to do the obvious. Common sense tells you to listen when your boss is talking to you, to speak softly in emotional situations, and to eliminate a danger in the office or factory. But what do you do if the decision you have to make has no obvious answer? How do you use common sense in making such a decision? Would it be wise to consider the feelings, thoughts, and experiences that constitute your common sense, just as you would with intuition? These are difficult questions to answer. More important, they show that making decisions based on common sense is not as simple as some people claim it to be.

There are two distinguishing characteristics of the common sense approach to decision making. First, decision makers who rely on common sense are capable of expressing themselves clearly and effectively on most of the factors that will influence their decisions. They do not rely primarily on instinct, intuition, or tradition. They understand how they make decisions and know why they do what they do. Second, they do not use any of the analytical approaches that can be applied to problems that are complex and difficult to solve.

Common sense is often called sound practical judgment. Judgment is that untheoretical and seemingly intuitive reaction to questions that are presented without much warning and to which almost immediate responses are demanded. Yet judgment apparently grows through experience. Persons who have been through a particular experience more than once are more likely to use good judgment in making a decision on a similar perplexing situation than persons who are faced with it for the first time.

You may be said to be using common sense if you make a simple comparison of costs and benefits on a course of action you're considering and decide—without calculating or computing—that the costs obviously outweigh the benefits.

Sound Decisions

Every decision maker hopes that the decisions he or she makes are sound ones. For a decision to be sound, the decision maker must have a deep understanding of the factors involved in the decision. If a first-line marketing manager, for example, is selecting among alternative ways of getting more vendors to carry the company's product line, that decision will be sound to the extent that the manager understands the market for the product line and the nature, needs, situations, and hopes of the vendors of such products. Some experts on decision making go so far as to say that once the details of a subject are completely mastered, decisions come naturally. Apart from such understanding, the soundness of a decision depends on some or all of the following abilities: interpreting data by converting them to information, drawing conclusions from data, applying imagination, being objective, and having patience.

Yet you should never assume that sound decisions will always result from using proper procedures. Judgment must be reckoned with. Judgment, moreover, is influenced by factors peculiar to the decision maker and to the company. Such factors include previous personal experience, preferences, inclinations, and authority. For instance, if a supervisor has a decision to make on which model of word processor to buy for the office, he or she may have narrowed the choice down to one made by ABC Company or one made by XYZ Company. The ABC Company is a leader in the field, while the XYZ Company is a little-known manufacturer. After comparing costs, capabilities, and potentials, the supervisor determines that the word processor made by XYZ Company is really better for the purposes to which it will be put. However, he or she recognizes that the ABC model is a safer choice. If it doesn't work out, the supervisor's boss will blame ABC Company, whereas if he or she buys XYZ Company's processor, the boss can blame him or her for not buying the best.

Decision makers are sometimes faced with making determinations that favor the interests of some and are contrary to the interests of others. The attitude of the decision maker rules when such value judgments are being made. You may be influenced to overrule all other considerations for any one or more of the following reasons: devotion to duty, a personal obligation, brotherhood, self-interest, moral responsibility, cultural preference, whim, efficiency, and others. Furthermore, when you make such a value judgment, you may express your preferences in a ranking order.

Although great value is placed on personal experience and natural aptitude when making decisions, these qualities are not always sufficient to ensure good choices. Higher-level managers and supervisors are sometimes faced with the problem of too much inconclusive information and not enough conclusive information. They must constantly deal with conflict of one sort or another with their peers, and they are often pressured by outside interests. In addition, they are human and fallible, not to forget emotional (at least to some degree). It would seem that they need some kind of system to be orderly and more exact in making decisions. The odds are that some of the more experienced and adept decision makers are following a definite procedure that they long ago incorporated into their particular techniques. It is true that with tough or complex problems to solve, you have to adopt the principles and procedures of study, investigation, recognition of alternatives, and selection of the alternative that will most likely give you the result you are looking for.

Psychologists say that when you have some tough decisions to make, don't try to make them at the end of the day. Late in the day your outlook is likely to be affected by fatigue, you may pass some factor off as trivial, and your decision may be biased. Postpone any decision making until the next day when you are fresh and can face facts with a positive and optimistic view. Chances are you will see the problem in a different light and, as a result, come up with a much better decision.

Credibility

A credibility problem in business or industry can do as much as anything to decrease efficiency and lower morale. Once a first-line manager loses credibility with employees, what he or she says may be disbelieved; just as bad if not worse, his or her decisions may be questioned or ignored. Credibility can be lost for several reasons. Some of the most common are: not knowing what's going on or what's coming up, not caring, and not knowing what to do. Of course, there are many variations of these acts of omission—all of which result in a loss of credibility.

Although credibility is usually difficult to regain, the effort should always be made to do so. It takes constant vigilance and hard work, including close attention to personal behavorial patterns and human relations principles. But suppose you feel that you simply need to improve your credibility. How should you proceed? Here is how to go about it:

• Carefully follow the policies and rules in your company. They were established to provide consistent and fair treatment of all employees. You must set the example in obeying them. If you take a shortcut, ignore a rule, or find a devious way to get around it, you lose not only credibility but respect as well.

• Be honest and truthful. It's very easy to be dishonest by bending the truth just a little or by covering up something that was handled improperly. Remember that nothing contributes to the loss of credibility more than dishonesty. If you cheat, then your people will cheat.

• Deal frankly and openly with others whenever possible. Although there will be occasions when you cannot share something with another person, in most instances, you can level with a person and tell him or her the real reason why you can or cannot do something. Avoid giving somebody a fabricated answer. People know when they're not receiving a straight answer, and your credibility will suffer.

• Always keep your promises. You can avoid unintentionally failing to keep them by making a note of a request or using some kind of follow-up procedure. But you're likely to get in trouble if you agree to do too much or promise to do something that someone else should do.

• Adopt and practice the golden rule. If you treat people the way you would like them to treat you, in a sincere manner, you'll get results. Keep this in mind the next time you make a decision involving one or more of your people.

• Do a good job of communicating by keeping people informed. The easiest way to do this is to hold periodic meetings with your people to keep them up to date. In this way, you can also let them know about upcoming changes. Such communication both builds credibility and helps improve employee morale, especially if you advise people of your plans and goals.

• Be systematic. Disorganization hurts credibility. The reliability of information and the logic of decisions are questioned when they are received from someone who is confused and unorganized. When you stay organized, you are stronger and in better control.

• Stress accuracy and correctness with your work. Both build credibility. If you make statements based mainly on opinion, your credibility may be questioned. If your reports contain numerous errors, you lose credibility.

• Keep on schedule. If you are late in completing a project or getting out a report, you create problems for everyone. People may begin to wonder if your schedule means anything. You must stay on target with everything you do.

• Stay on top of your specialty. You perform an important function in your company, and people expect you to be an expert at what you do. If you fall behind or don't have the right answers, you'll soon get a reputation for not knowing what you're doing, and with that will go your credibility.

Experience

Everyone learns from experience, and the experience does not have to be your own. All you need to benefit from experience is to have a good memory and know where you can learn the experiences of others. When you can't draw on experience for one reason or another and you need to make a decision, the only thing you can do is experiment or try something.

An experiment can be defined as a tentative procedure or policy. But experimenting can be quite costly compared to the cost of using existing data and information. It is, therefore, understandable why decision makers like to rely on experience whenever they can. Unfortunately, there are some problems with it.

Far too much reliance is placed today on the memories of key people in an organization, particularly engineering and maintenance people. Individuals are not only capable of making a mistake, they are mortal and can leave the organization. They can die or change jobs and take valuable unrecorded experience with them.

Another problem is that it is not enough to keep records of good experiences and decisions. It is equally important to record bad ones. While decision makers may not be proud of their indiscretions, records of them serve as reminders and warnings. All of us should assume that mistakes were made and failures occurred when good decision makers went astray. If not warned, good decision makers might go astray again.

Some managers, including supervisors, handle their jobs as if they were working only for their departments and not for their companies. They may or may not realize it, but keeping their operations secret could be costing their companies money as well as depriving the companies of the benefits that can be derived from learning the experiences of others. Someone in every department should have complete access to the records, files, and experiences of every other department in all matters of mutual concern. This responsibility may be divided, but it should be known.

No company should tolerate private files of company data, but such conditions exist when insecure persons try to make themselves indispensable by hoarding information that should be available to others. Such individuals hope to increase their importance by making others come to them or be dependent upon them for various data and information. Some limits should be set on what constitutes personal or private data. Experience and information that cannot be easily retrieved is not available for the person who needs it.

There is no question that the more experienced supervisors are, the easier it is for them to make good decisions—provided, of course, that they have learned from that experience. While good experiences are most easily remembered, bad ones may be forgotten. It's human to want to put your mistakes out of your mind.

You can learn from a mistake if you take the time to think about your error rather than just dismissing it as an unfortunate occurrence. Treat a mistake as a problem and realize that you need to understand the problem before you can solve it. Try going through a questioning procedure regarding the cause. You'll find that this will help you not to make that mistake a second time. This is the way you learn by experience.

The Problem of Time

It seems that first-line managers will always have the problem of "not having enough time to do everything I would like to do." Yet often, they have only themselves to blame because they have not learned how to make the best use of time.

Wasting time is one of our most costly activities, despite the fact that each of us can do something about it if we try. When time is wasted, it is gone forever. There is no such thing as "not enough time." If you feel that you are too busy, look at the people who are busier than you and still get more accomplished. The same amount of time is available to all of us—some just use their time better.

Since time is so valuable, we should figure out the best way to get the most from what is available to us. A few minutes each morning devoted to planning our day can make us much more efficient as well as increase the amount of things we can get done. We would also have more time for some of the decisions we must make that require study and thought. Here are some suggestions on how to make the best use of your time:

• Make time work for you. Adopting timesaving habits is the way to go about making time work for you. You do it by starting right in the morning—getting up when the alarm rings (or earlier) and getting to work on time. A time-conscious supervisor is usually on the job long before his or her people. Once you begin being punctual in starting your day, other habits of effective use of time will fall into place. You'll make sure you're on time for appointments and meetings. You'll avoid dawdling at tasks that can be done quickly and without much effort. Punctuality will become a way of life. You will have made time work for you.

• Overcome slow starts. If you are a slow starter, you undoubtedly waste much valuable time. You can overcome this problem by planning your work the night before so that you don't have to make decisions the first thing in the morning when you haven't yet shifted into high gear. Another trick the acknowledged slow starter can pull to get himself or herself on the road is to have the day begin with a meeting or an appointment. The obligation to contribute, participate, and necessarily be alert will help to overcome his or her morning inertia.

You can use some psychology with a subordinate who finds it difficult to get started on the job. In the afternoon, give the person an assignment that he or she can make a good start on but not finish that day. The person will pick it up the next morning and have an easier time getting going for the day.

• Decide what to do first. Start with the job that is most on your mind. This is simply good reasoning. Your effectiveness and efficiency are poor when you are concerned or worried, so it's logical that you should try to relieve such feelings as soon as you can. When you have done so, you will be able to do a better job on your other tasks. You may have a tough decision to make. Or you may have planned to talk to one of your subordinates, and what you have to say is bothering you because you need to reprimand him or her. After you have handled this matter, you will be better able to keep your mind on other work.

• Tackle the job that someone has requested of you. Your boss, naturally, should be considered first. In fact, doing jobs that your boss has requested should in most cases take priority over all jobs that you need to do. After satisfying him or her, you'll want to give attention to jobs that your peers and your people have asked for. The jobs that need to be done to satisfy only yourself should be your last choice.

• Plan your work. Almost any system that enables you to use time effectively requires that you plan. Since planning involves thinking, choosing, and making decisions, your memory may be taxed to keep things straight and in order. Making a list gets around this and enables you to plan efficiently. Preparing a list of the jobs you have to do and the things you want to do helps you to compare importance, set priorities, and put jobs in order.

A list also has a motivating effect, in that you can be moved to get a job done so that it can be crossed off. Once you've crossed off a few items that you had to handle, your conscience won't bother you as much when you do some of the things you want to do. You might say that this is using psychology on yourself, but if it works, who's to say it shouldn't be done? Start listing and crossing off. You'll get more satisfaction from accomplishment, and you'll be doing more of the things that the boss hasn't asked you to do but that you know must be done.

National surveys have revealed that organizations can blame a big share of their poor profits on the laxity of their employees—a laxity that shows in lateness and wasting time on the job. The poor profits result from not getting from the employees work that is paid for. Much of the wasted time occurs simply because people are not punctual. How do your people stack up in this respect? Do all of them begin working promptly at their starting time in the morning, or are there some who are still talking about last night's game ten minutes after? How many of your people take only the lunchtime they're entitled to?

You might say that a few minutes lost by being late now and then doesn't add up to much, but let's look at some figures to see just how much lost time costs. If each one of your company's people makes $10 an hour, and there are 100 employees in your company who are late or waste 15 minutes in a working day, the total loss in a year to your company is $65,000. If your company has 1,000 employees, the annual loss is more than half a million dollars!

The theft of time costs industry more than $35 billion a year. The "stealing" includes late starts and early quits, long lunch periods, taking sick days when not sick, and doing personal work on the job.

If you are aware of the importance of time, you should have no trouble answering the question, "What part of your job takes the most time?" Also, you probably know about the long, time-consuming jobs your people do and wish that you could shorten those tasks.

Study those long jobs by breaking them up into their components. Look at each one to see if it truly is a necessary part of the whole job. What would happen if a step were shortened or omitted entirely? Can two steps be combined so that they're done simultaneously? Continue looking until you find a step or two that you can do something about.

You and your people should also periodically review your work procedures to make sure you're not doing a job the roundabout way simply because you've always done it that way. Furthermore, if you come across a better and quicker way of doing a certain job, look around for other areas where the same procedure might apply. Make job simplification one of your goals, and get your people involved. The field is wide open for you to come up with time- and money-saving ideas.

The Value of Quick Thinking

Supervisors often find themselves in situations where they must make a quick decision. Demanding management, impatient workers, and sensitive production processes may and do require their immediate attention at any time. Furthermore, management and society may demand that their judgments on these matters be right more often than wrong. In many cases, they cannot avoid deciding, not can they call for more time.

Almost all decisions that first-line managers make are affected by the time factor. Of concern is the diminishing effectiveness of a decision with the passing of time. In addition, it is easy to lose sight of your objective when you are under any kind of pressure. Since time is usually the reason for pressure, your best bet is to try for as much time as you can get. You need to look over a situation to determine whether you really must come up with a decision quickly or whether only the person presenting the problem to you feels that you must. A problem sometimes appears worse than it is; inexperienced people and people not familiar with a particular condition may view it with unwarranted alarm. Then, too, many people are impatient when things are not going their way.

Few supervisors are not bothered by having to make a decision quickly or under pressure. Yet you can be more sure of making a good decision if you can take the time to get facts, consider them, and choose between alternatives. The reduction of elements to a minimum and the conversion of variables into constants are vital if good decisions and judgments are to be made. How you handle these functions determines how effective you are on the job and how quickly you move up in the company to a position of greater responsibility.

The ability to think quickly comes naturally to a few people, but most of us develop the skill over a period of time in which we gain experience and build up our memory. Although a retentive memory and a near-total recall are associated with alertness or quickness, the skills can actually be attributed to a very agile mind. Memory is more related to learning ability and concentration than it is to general intelligence. If you have an average mental capacity but a strong desire to learn, you can improve your memory capability. When you incorporate rewards and punishment in your program, you do even better. We remember best the things we have tried hardest to remember.

While good decision makers are never rash and impetuous in resolving issues, much less are they procrastinators. What may appear to be deliberation may be a manifestation of incompetence. One of the most apparent characteristics of good decision makers is the spontaneity and quickness with which they will make decisions once they've analyzed all elements. If they are competent, knowledgeable in the principles of management and human relations, and understand the company's goals, there is seldom a need for excessive delay in reaching a decision. It is therefore highly probable that the so-called caution of many decision makers is a blend of fear, lack of application, and incompetence.

By selectively committing specific information to memory, you can prepare yourself for the day when you need to come up with a quick decision. First-line managers who do a good job of memorizing sections of the union contract, for example, are in an excellent position to handle labor disputes expeditiously and effectively. Not only are they able to dispose of matters with authority, they also enhance their reputation for wide-ranging intelligence and knowledge, thus gaining the respect of both their people and their superiors.

Similar to the person whose mind has total recall capabilities is the person whose mind enables him or her to answer specific questions without hesitation. The instant response is what is really amazing about such a person because this is a test under the pressure of time. To do well in such circumstances requires not only a good memory but also an at-ease nature, an ability to think and reason quickly, and a mental attitude that precludes becoming easily rattled.

Likewise, the person who can perform rapid calculations in his or her head is often accorded special status. In some circles, the person is labeled a genius. Nobody cares whether the person can't get along with people or isn't perceptive, and there is no assurance that he or she will be good at handling human relations problems. In this respect, the "genius" would probably not make a good supervisor.

Those who recognize their limitations in mental gymnastics and realize they will never be quick thinkers must hold their own or gain an advantage by applying substiutue techniques. Most of us are in this class, although we may not be aware of it. In place of quick thinking, we substitute meditative or reflective action, or we become noncommittal. We may, for example, listen carefully and occasionally interject comments that are merely restatements of what another person is saying. Words of simple understanding and empathy take the place of any judgment. When listening, we may search for insight or self-analysis on the part of the other person. This can then be complimented and promoted to get the person to understand his or her position. Once this is done, we can proceed to a solution of the problem. Thus what might appear to be a quick response to a problem is simply a mutual discussion of it.

Developing Quick Thinking

You can become adept at quick thinking, but it will not be easy for you unless you have a need for the skill. The person on the job or in an environment where he or she is seldom called upon to make an immediate judgment will not become proficient in that skill because the need for it is so infrequent. But this is not to say that a person should not recognize that snap judgments will be required of him or her occasionally and that preparation for them would pay off. Such reasoning is most applicable in situations where protecting one's own interests is very important to the person.

Many first-line managers are familiar with the worker who, seemingly on the spur of the moment, devises a new way of getting a job done. With work that requires hand coordination and motor skills, the variety of procedures that can be found is surprisingly large. Efficiency experts who have studied a particular job are often outguessed by a quick-thinking worker. Such an incident simply illustrates the fact that the average person will, consciously or unconsciously, do what seems best to take care of his or her own interests.

You can become skilled in what appears to be quick thinking by establishing procedures to be followed to handle problems similar to ones that came up in the past on the expectation that they will probably come up again. Such planning easily gets around the need for quick thinking of an original nature. Probably the most common example of this principle is an ordinary fire drill. An often recognized advantage of such training is that the actual incident, when it occurs, is handled routinely and as matter-of-factly as if it were "just another fire drill." As a result, it is carried out efficently and effectively. Similar success can be achieved in the office or factory when the likelihood of certain events occurring is recognized and procedures are established for what to do when they happen. Spill prevention and control in an industrial plant is a good example. The supervisor who knows what to do and how to do it is helped in a situation that, in the absence of foresight, could be very stressful. In some companies, supervisors are taught how to handle employee's grievances and disruptive behavior by acting out the roles of both parties in training classes. Once having experienced such a situation, the supervisor doesn't later lose his or her composure when a similar problem arises on the job.

There are other ways to become skilled in thinking fast or appearing to—although, on close examination, they are simply stratagems to give you thinking time. A few examples are:

• Adopt some personal mannerisms, such as gazing up at the celling or looking intently at the floor, closing your eyes, steepling your fingers, and pursing your mouth. It's best that you do something you might normally do on other occasions.

• Ask questions, even though they may have already been answered. In addition to giving you time to think, you may learn something new.

• Learn to use delaying sentences. Typical ones are, "This can be handled in more than one way"; "I've thought quite a bit about this"; and "Let's summarize what we've done to this point."

In developing the skill of quick thinking, two attributes make the task easier. One is to have some memory or related experience to draw upon. The other is to be able to adapt memories and experiences to a new problem or situation. Yet a young person lacking these attributes may still demonstrate the ability to think quickly. An explanation may be that the young person is more alert and less likely to be distracted by previous frustrations or defeats.

In contrast, boldness, coupled with inexperience and irresponsibility, can lead to serious mistakes. An older person with experience is likely to be more cautious and hesitant, knowing that mistakes and errors can thus be avoided. Skill in the two attributes can enable a supervisor who has been on the job for many years to recognize and handle a serious situation quickly and effectively. If you were to ask this person how he or she was able to do it, you very probably would hear, "I faced a similar situation some time ago and didn't do so well with it, so I figured out what I would do if the problem came up again. When it eventually did, I knew just what to do, and it was right."

Snap Decisions

You must not take your decisions lightly if you want them to be sure to hold up. Some degree of effort and thought should be put into every decision, including those that are made quickly. A sign of an inept decision maker is making snap decisions when they aren't necessary.

Even though your batting average might be very good, it could be better if the first answer or solution to a problem that comes to mind isn't adopted. A corollary to resisting impulsive action states that even good decisions may be rejected if they are proposed at one wrong time or are proposed with such aggressiveness that they generate resistance. Everyone resists change to some degree, and everyone is negative in some respect. We show it when an idea or an answer to a problem is offered us. Except when what is proposed is exactly what we want or hope for, we tend to look for reasons to oppose or reject it.

How does a person become proficient in making quick decisions if the process is stressful as well as risky? It would seem that the learning period would be difficult and at times embarrassing. Not necessarily so. Practical experience in quick thinking can be developed through alertness, observation, and practice.

Essentially, you must become very knowledgeable about the technical details of your environment. Every detail, however minute, and every incident on the job may someday be relevant to a future problem. A new or inexperienced first-line manager should be as curious and inquisitive as he or she can be about all the operations in the work area. This includes talking to experienced managers about their decisions. It also includes looking for relationships between apparently unlike situations.

It is easier for a supervisor to give a quick answer to a question when he or she has been forewarned. If, for example, you have heard that your boss is going to ask you how many times a critical machine in the department broke down in the past year and expect you to know the answer, you can immediately check the records so that you'll be able to give him or her a quick reply. Of course, this may not happen often, since seldom are you made aware in advance of questions you'll be asked. But it pays to be prepared. You should train yourself to react rapidly and depend upon your own good judgment to make a quick decision when you are called upon to do so. The manager who can do this without hesitating is looked upon with respect, whereas a slow thinker is either ignored or pitied.

Learn to recognize when snap judgment is necessary and when it is not. This enables you to minimize the amount of quick thinking you must do. As a result, more of your decisions will be good ones. There is no real advantage (and there are many disadvantages) to making a snap judgment when you have time to do a thorough study.

Practicing making snap decisions but not implementing them is a good way to become skilled in the art without suffering damage if you are wrong. You can make this a game of sorts, and by keeping records you can see whether the quality of your decision making improves with time. The person who can think quickly and be right most of the time is a valuable asset to his or her company.

Planning Helps Decision Making

The procedure of planning helps first-line managers in making decisions. If several courses of action are possible on a problem, you must think through the advantages and disadvantages of each. Reasoning and evaluation skills are developed in the process. Although you may see the need to plan and the advantages of doing so, you must also recognize that you have to be able to implement the plans you make. If they are impractical or very difficult to carry out, they may not be of much value. Therefore, you should make sure your plans are logical and practical.

What are the requirements of a good plan? It should encompass and include the following:

• It should be specific rather than general. The more explicit it is, the less chance there is for it to be misinterpreted or misapplied. Objectives and goals should be clearly defined. The means for carrying out the plan should be indicated.

• It should distinguish between the known and the unknown so that both are given proper consideration. The probable effects of the unknown should be estimated. Planning should be more than just anticipation and reaction.

• It should be based on facts. The more facts it is based on, the better it is. If facts are not available, then reasonable, sound judgments must be made. Intelligent thinking should serve as the foundation for a plan.

• It must be flexible and capable of being modified. No plan is infallible, nor can it cover all possible contigencies. Conditions under which a plan will be most effective change, as do the variables and factors on which the plan is based.

• It must be acceptable to the persons who adopt it and to those who are affected by it. Acceptable implies that there is a willingness to participate and cooperate in carrying it out and a willingness to take the consquences. Plans must be consistent with the aims and goals of the company and the way it conducts its business.

The most proficient planners have imagination as well as creative ability. An effective planner usually has a good balance between optimism and pessimism and a practical as well as realistic viewpoint. Planning involves forecasting, and although mathematical and statistical techniques are used in forecasting, hunch and intuition often play a part. Experience, of course, is a big aid to any planning effort.

Speed in Making Decisions

A decision has to be made, and you are expected to make it. How fast do you act if it is not a critical decision? Making a decision quickly without reasonable grounds for delay does have an advantage, in that you gain time; in some situations, time is very important. Frequently, you'll find that the decision you make right off the bat is as good as the one you make after you put the problem aside for a while to think about it. A quick decision also gives you a longer period of time to correct the occasional decision that goes wrong. When you postpone some decisions, you eventually get to the point where they can't be reversed.

How you handle many decisions depends on whether you are impulsive or thoughtful—whether you're reactive or reflective. A reflective person will take time to consider alternative courses so as not to risk an error. But taking too much time is the hallmark of a poor decision maker. The impulsive individual has very little anxiety about making a mistake and so seldom hesitates. Yet the impulsive person is no better a decision maker, since too many errors are made because of haste. The best decision maker is one who is able to decide impulsively without making mistakes. Attaining that ideal is difficult for most of us.

There's no relationship between impulsiveness and intelligence. Extremes of both are found in the most astute and highly educated people. However, the nervous or temperamental person may be inclined to be more impulsive than the calm and cautious person. Creative and innovative people also tend to be quick-acting.

Suppose you feel that your decision-making style is too strong in one direction. What can you do to change? If you believe you're too impulsive, you can force yourself to hold up on the quick answer or fast decision you usually make. Count to 100, say, before you respond (thinking, of course, along the way). If you are a strongly reflective person, you probably will have a more difficult time changing because you will be forcing yourself to decide before you're sure. Try giving yourself a time limit, and when that is up, make your decision.

Tricks to Avoid Making Decisions

Some first-line managers will do almost anything to avoid making a decision, and many have found devious ways of doing it. How is it done? Here are some popular avoidance tactics:

• Say that the timing isn't right. This is a favorite dodge of people who feel they are on the spot. Fortunately for them, many decisions have deadlines beyond which no action can be taken or that tend to maintain the status quo. Thus, the technique amounts to doing nothing and letting time run out. A variation of this is to give the matter a low priority. Then it can legitimately be ignored in favor of more important things.

• Come up with a diversionary move. Faced with a yes-or-no decision and with the possibility of making a mistake, a decision maker may suggest that he or she work on another important project. Anything that will take a person's mind off a problem will often suffice.

• Take a day off. Instead of aggressively tackling a problem they know is coming up, some supervisors may take a "sick" day or ask for a few days of vacation. The excuses may vary with the person and his or her inclinations, but they all amount to the same thing: ducking a decision.

• Pass the buck. Good managers appreciate the need to properly delegate matters and duties, but this should never be done with a responsibility that is rightfully theirs. It may only take a few such incidents to convince the manager's superiors that another manager should be hired to replace the weak, "no-guts" one.

• Follow tradition. A decision to change something can be avoided by claiming, "The job has always been done that way, and it has worked" or "That's the way we've always handled such a problem." This is fine if the supervisor can ignore technological progress, rising costs, competition, and many other factors that rule out such hidebound thinking.

• Refer to the policy manual. With this approach, a first-line

118

manager is seemingly making a decision, yet the only skill required is the ability to read the index of the company manual. Of course, the manager can also claim that following company policy is the best course of action for any decision he or she makes. Considering that it is not possible to cover every problem with a policy, when a supervisor is called upon to make a decision not covered by one, he or she can always look for a management precedent. This would consist of what others have done in the past in similar and preferably identical situations.

• Have a committee appointed. Although most first-line managers seldom have to face a problem of such complexity or magnitude that their boss would accept such a ploy, stranger things have happened. This, of course, is a common way of shifting the responsibility for a decision to others. Granted, it makes maximum use of expertise. But it also has the convenient feature that by the time the problem is studied, it will have been forgotten or management will have decided that it's not worth the effort. A variation of the committee approach is for the supervisor to claim that the decision is too important for him or her to make. This is a potentially risky way to avoid deciding because you must pass the decision making to your boss without giving the impression of being indecisive or of lacking the authority to make it.

Chapter Five

Communication: Key to Making Decisions

A first-line manager spends a large percentage of his or her time transmitting ideas, information, and instructions to others, orally and in writing. This communication process is essentially the way the responsibilities of a manager are carried out. The procedure, however, is not without its difficulties. Most communication problems fall into three basic groups.

- The technical problem of the language, the conventions, and the way messages are transmitted.
- The semantic problem of the language and conventions conveying the desired meaning.
- The effectiveness problem of how meaning brings about the desired results.

Cybernetics is involved in the technical functions of communications. Cybernetics is the science of communication and control theory that is concerned especially with the comparative study of automatic control systems (such as the nervous system and brain and mechanical-electrical communication systems). In cybernetics, information has no relationship to meaning. It is a quantitative measure of the amount of order in a system and is related not to what you *do* say but to what you *can* say about a matter. The more probable a message is, the less information it gives. If a supervisor always tells the boss "Everything is going well," the boss can predict those words before he or she hears them and thus receives no information.

Communications experts point out that in trying to get our ideas across to others, we often encounter transmission problems such as poor reception and interference. Poor reception occurs when a manager gives an order that an employee didn't expect and isn't prepared for. Interference takes place when a manager gives conflicting instructions; any interference in the receipt of a message increases uncertainty. Only through communicating skillfully can a manager avoid these human transmission failures.

The meaning that a message has to the receiver is a matter of semantics. A person may say one thing but the receiver may hear something different, even if the word sent and the word received are exactly the same. A number of factors are involved:

- The environment or situation in which the communication takes place.
- The similarity between the past experiences of the sender and those of the receiver.
- The distinction between facts and opinions.
- The degree of abstractness of the conventions used.
- The complexity of the expressions and words used.

Usually, the more direct the communication, the more effective it will be. A problem arises in some companies in that the number of levels of management through which a message passes affects the action that is finally taken. The effectiveness of a communication depends both on efficient transmission of a message and on understanding of its meaning. The degree of acceptance of the communication is an indication of its effectiveness.

How communications are accepted by receivers depends on their needs, past experiences, and readiness for the message. People tend to hear what they want to hear and to reject what they don't want to hear. Usually, they will accept a communication if it doesn't conflict with their goals. If people feel that they are part of a well-organized working team, they will tend to accept many communications without consciously questioning them.

Communicating Information

First-line managers continually need information in order to make on-the-job decisions. Most of what they need is at hand or can be obtained from subordinates, peers, and superiors. Some is self-generated, and a small amount may come from outside the company.

If you were to examine the various bits of information that flow to a first-line manager and are needed by him or her to carry out the job functions, you would find that the information encompasses a wide range of different activities. But since most subordinates try to be helpful in addition to seeking promotion, they may originate as well as pass on quite a few facts that they think their boss should have. People who are active and in pursuit of goals seem to have a strong desire to report news and information in many ways and forms.

A lack of information on certain subjects means only that it is not available. It doesn't mean that it is not needed. While the scarcity of information may complicate your job and occasionally make it difficult, duplication, overlaps, and the retention of inconsequential and routine documents can slow the retrieval of it. The large number of legal and certified documents, engineering drawings, financial reports, and operating specifications that most companies create have brought on filing and storage problems. However, microfilming and electronic data processing are making inroads in these areas.

New supervisors soon learn that there is more to their job than simply making decisions. The decisions must be implemented. It is when communicating them that they often run into difficulties. In order to have their decisions carried out, they must communicate their content and purpose. To do this, they must verify that their intentions and the reasons for them are received and correctly understood. Verification is not easy. People readily change jobs, and new employees have different work backgrounds. Add to this the fact that many managers do not communicate as well as they think they do. Yet it is necessary that decisions or directions be understood before any attempt is made to carry them out.

Before you ask employees to carry out your decision, you need to get them involved to the extent that they feel they are "in it" with you and will be part of its accomplishment. You must do this in a manner such that they do not feel that you regard them as untrustworthy or not very smart. You must show, too, that you have faith in them and their abilities. If you are unable to impart these feelings, your relationship with your people will suffer, not just with respect to the decision of the moment, but with respect to all decisions.

Verifying That You're Understood

There are a variety of methods for determining whether you've communicated well and your decision has been understood. You would be well advised to use most if not all of them to verify that your people understand before they start carrying out a decision or begin work on a hazardous, major, or complex job. Here is how to do that:

• Ask them if they understand. Although this is the most frequently used method, it is certainly not the best. Few employees feel comfortable in admitting they do not understand directions given by their boss. As a result, the positive nod of the head to "Do you understand?" has gotten more supervisors in trouble than any other response. What has happened is that decisions have been carried out incorrectly or not at all. Except for people you have worked with a long time or in low-risk situations, you are better off using a different method.

• Have them repeat your directions. Don't be concerned that they will think you don't trust them. This may be true only if you use the method with every little direction you give. If employed sparingly, especially when communication is vital, such as when safety is at stake, it is a good procedure.

• Ask them about key points. Effective implementation of decisions often hinges on a key step or point. Rather than have all your directions repeated, it's more practical as well as more effective to ask only about the key point. For example, if you've given a lot of directions to a subordinate on the preparation of a report, ask the subordinate to confirm only the date that you said the report was due.

• Ask a question about procedure. How well a person understands the way a job is to be done can be demonstrated by what steps he or she intends to take to do it. Rather than focusing directly on the decision to get the job done, determine the extent of understanding from the person's plan of action. A side benefit from this method is that the person will be made to feel more "in" on the decision by explaining his or her intentions.

• Have them paraphrase your directions. By having the person feed back your directions in his or her *own* words, you can check for accuracy and understanding. In addition, ownership of the decision is increased when the person puts it in his or her own words. The only problem with this method is that it is not natural to restate in another form someone else's words. If you have many situations where accurate communications are required, it may be worthwhile to train people to paraphrase, because it is probably the most accurate verification technique.

• Have them explain your directions to someone else. This method of communicating is appropriate when more than one person is involved in carrying out a decision. You can listen to the explanation and add encouragement if it is correct. Should the person doing the explaining leave out something important, you can add it. By having one employee explain something to another, they both become more involved. Not only that, but the chance to share directions verbally may strengthen commitment to carrying out the decision.

You may wonder whether employees will become suspicious if you start using these methods of communicating, especially if you adopt one or more every time you give directions. The solution to this is to introduce techniques slowly and in the right situations. When they are used cautiously and correctly, few employees will become concerned or disturbed. You may find that as you begin to favor verification methods, your people will start using them also. This will improve communications and decision effectiveness throughout your department.

Informal Communications

All organizations develop various methods of formal internal communication. Generally, these take the form of policies, standard practices, specifications and schedules, and the like. Several of these formal means of communicating have already been discussed in earlier chapters of this book.

However, many communications are informal in nature, one such type being the "grapevine." The grapevine primarily serves the social needs of employees in a company, yet it is often helpful for the attainment of organizational goals. First-line managers can use the grapevine as an aid in making decisions, but they should not accept rumors, gossip, and other negative forms of communication for the same purpose. Since the grapevine can never be destroyed, it should always be taken into consideration when communicating within an organization. Making a remark at an opportune time may alleviate a stressful situation or remedy a disciplinary problem without the need to reprimand someone.

Clever supervisors sometimes get things done by planting information in the office grapevine. But if you decide to use this informal way of communicating, you should be aware of its pitfalls. Here are some guidelines in that respect:

- Never resort to the grapevine with a malicious purpose in mind. Such tactics are strictly taboo; you could easily lose your credibility.
- Hold up on using the grapevine if you can get your message across with standard procedures. Make sure you understand the situation, the people involved, and what can happen if your attempt fails.
- Avoid letting the grapevine control you. Don't allow subordinates to use the grapevine to draw you into their way of thinking.
- Learn who the grapevine pushers are and how news travels. There may be more than one channel of communications.
- Be aware of other grapevines in the company. Top management grapevines are complex and dangerous.

The grapevine is popular because everyone likes to be in on a secret or to know about something before it happens. But it shouldn't be trusted. It works about the same as that game where one person whispers a message to another, who, in turn, passes it on to another. The last person getting the message finds it to be quite different from the original version.

Within a company, loose talk can be deadly and can sometimes cause personal harm. For example, an employee may overhear part of a conversation, pass it along the grapevine, and before you know it, people are talking about personnel layoffs and shake-ups, policy changes, and company losses. The result is worried workers, lower production outputs, poorer quality and service. Employees have been known to quit their company and seek other employment simply on the basis of a rumor.

Such things can happen in your department unless you take steps to stop rumors and gossip the only positive way known—get the facts and spread them. Here are a few questions you should ask yourself whenever you hear something via the grapevine:

- Is this harmful to the company or to one of the employees?
- Where did the rumor originate?
- Can it be verified?

By answering these questions, you may be able to check out the rumor's authenticity. Regardless, don't pass the rumor on. If you and others follow this advice, the grapevine will wither, at least for the moment.

Bypassing

Bypassing is the practice of going above your immediate boss to a higher-management person in order to make a point or gain a benefit. In most hierarchical organizations, this practice is considered a "no-no," even though you may feel that your communication will have more impact or that you will get better or quicker results. Management and personnel experts say that bypassing your boss may work when there is no other way, but you shouldn't try it very often. It is a dangerous step, particularly in large organizations and companies. Managers taking such action violate the rules of corporate procedure relating to the chain of command. As a result, people in responsible positions become upset because their authority is challenged. Invariably, hard feelings develop and destroy good manager/subordinate relationships.

If you have never bypassed your boss, consider the possible reasons why you would want to do so. For instance, what if you felt that upper management was not aware of something that was happening in your department and that, if it was, action would certainly be taken. By today's rules of conduct, you should not call attention to this, since, in effect, you would be criticizing the boss's superior. Such criticism would not be taken lightly, especially if you are right and could prove it. You stand to lose both ways, whether you are right or wrong.

Another situation that you might think justifies bypassing your boss may be the one where a person in the department, such as a fellow supervisor, is not making good decisions and the boss knows it but won't do anything about it. You are not likely to effect a change in this situation either. The problem revolves around your boss's judgment. Management won't step in as long as the department's work is done on time and at a reasonable cost. Management sees each department as a unit; it doesn't look into a department's operation as long as it is running according to plan or achieving its profit goal.

Bypassing your boss is not recommended, regardless of how serious you feel a situation is. You have too much to lose compared to what you might gain. Although you might pull off the maneuver once, you could suffer a great loss if you tried it again.

Participation

Because of the increasing complexity of decisions being made in many companies and the rising desire for involvement and commitment on the part of subordinates, managers have been turning more and more to the practice of participative management. The theory rests on the assumptions that employees at all levels of an organization are capable of contributing usefully to the decision-making process and that, in general, this willingness and capability have not been used. Supporting the theory is the thinking of many managers that when subordinates are more involved in decision making, superiors have greater influence in how decisions are carried out.

However, this is a difficult thing for some first-line managers to accept, especially those who believe they have earned the privilege of making their own decisions because of the years of hard work, training, and sacrifices they have put in. Such managers don't realize that management is not a privilege but rather a responsibility. Subordinates should participate in decisions concerning their work. Other supervisors see participation as a shifting of responsibility. It certainly isn't that, because no one knows a particular job better than the person doing that job day after day. Some of the best ideas and solutions to problems come from the very people doing the work.

In any business, the power to make decisions must be vested in managerial personnel. A higher-level manager or a supervisor must be in a position to take decisive action quickly, and the person must be given definite responsibility to do so. In numerous instances today, when people affected by a change become involved in making the decisions that determine how it is to be implemented, they tend not to resist it. Yet this conclusion is not valid in all cases. The problem of how a supervisor can achieve participation can be complex because participation means different things to different supervisors. To some, it is a way to manipulate people to share a viewpoint already held by the supervisor. To others, it is merely a routine to be followed to create an illusion that the employees have some voice in what is happening to them. Of course, such thinking diverges widely from the true meaning of participation.

True participation cannot be achieved simply by asking people for it, nor can a first-line manager demand that employees join in. Real participation depends on the feelings and attitudes of the people involved. The act of asking people to attend a meeting to discuss a management problem is insufficient motivation to get them to participate.

Employees must *want* to participate, and they must believe that their supervisor is sincere and honest in his or her intention. They must believe, furthermore, that if their ideas have merit, there is a good likelihood that they will be accepted. For these beliefs to exist, there must be a good relationship between the supervisor and the employees based on mutual respect and trust. If these feelings are not present, then any request for participation would be viewed with suspicion and mistrust. In addition, a deterioration of the relationship could result.

Another prerequisite for successful participation is that the first-line manager must feel safe and secure in his or her position. Some managers may be reluctant to try to get participation from their people because of how they perceive their managerial role. A supervisor might, for instance, believe that to ask for advice or opinion from employees would be a sign of his or her inadequacy to handle the supervisory position. He or she might feel that any involvement of workers in making decisions that are considered the supervisor's responsibilities would risk his or her status as a supervisor. The truth of the matter, however, is that if employees are permitted and encouraged by their supervisor to participate, their respect for him or her often increases rather than decreases.

One more prerequisite for participation is absence of commitment on the supervisor's part to a certain course of action. The supervisor must be open to any and all alternatives. When people are invited to participate in making decisions, their ideas will both agree and disagree with those of their supervisor. Some of their ideas may be superior. If the supervisor is convinced from the beginning that his or her way of handling a problem is best and is the only way of accomplishing a change, then it would be wise for the supervisor not to try to involve others as participants in making the decision. Any such attempt would soon be recognized as meaningless, a waste of time, and even dishonest.

However, even when a first-line manager is committed to a particular course of action or a particular step, there will inevitably be some parts of the process that can be handled in a variety of ways, any one of which would be acceptable. Thus, the manager might choose one or more of these ways as the subject for participative decision making. In that manner, he or she can control the area of participation and yet gain some degree of personal involvement among those affected by the decision. An example of this would be a supervisor's decision to stagger the smoke breaks or lunch times of the people in his or her department. After explaining why the staggering is necessary, the supervisor would ask the people to select the particular times each would leave the job. Thus, the decisions regarding scheduling of the off-the-job times would be joint ones.

A final condition necessary for effective participation is the employees' willingness to express themselves and to offer suggestions once they have been encouraged to do so. Participation fails with people who are passive or reticent. Such feelings are usually a result either of their experiences on the job or their cultural beliefs.

If all of these conditions don't exist in the manager/employee situation and relationship, a manager should be very careful in considering the participation of his or her people in decision making. If, on the other hand, all the conditions are positive, the use of participation can result in significant benefits.

The Benefits of Participation

When employees participate in the decision-making process, both they and their company gain. Thus, it pays for first-line managers to encourage participation at every opportunity. A few such benefits are:

- Participation often serves to prevent worthless ideas from being adopted and poorly conceived changes from being made.
- The procedure helps to increase employees' confidence in management's intentions.
- When employees are asked to express their opinion, they feel important and "in" on things.
- Participation helps to develop a better understanding of change.
- Because of participation, people become more committed to the decision in which they took part.
- When subordinates participate, their capabilities are developed and expanded.
- Participation helps employees to broaden their outlook.

The Problems with Participative Decision Making

Not everyone agrees that participative and group decision making is good; in fact, several groups oppose it. Some educators and writers are against it because they feel it tends to destroy individualism. They say that group decision making promotes conformity and causes people to avoid thinking for themselves—it is easy to go along with the group's opinion.

Another category of people not in favor of participative or group decision making are those who have been trained and have experience in the scientific approach. Their laboratory research has been conducted systematically and has led them to make decisions that way. They believe that when a group of persons, some informed and others uninformed, attempt to contribute toward making a decision, they will fail miserably. The best decisions are made, these people feel, by those who are trained and informed.

Mathematically inclined people also usually oppose participative decision making. They are at a loss to understand how most people could possibly apply mathematics effectively. They point out that the best approach to specifying and consequently solving a problem is to construct a mathematical model of it. The model will eliminate superfluous and confusing variables; and most likely, the problem can be stated in a way that will permit use of the computer, thus adding speed and accuracy in reaching a decision.

Meetings

Meetings are probably the best means of communicating with your people, provided there are no surprises when it comes to asking your people to participate. You should do your best to let them know before the meeting if they will be called upon in any special way. Tell them what to expect. Even a few minutes advanced notice to think about the meeting is helpful to most people. Say something like "This afternoon we're going to get together for a few minutes to talk about what capabilities we should have with the computer we're planning to bring into the department. So think about it between now and then." In the meeting, ask for volunteers whenever you can. Never force your people to participate, and handle shy people very carefully.

Listed below are some benefits that come from getting together with your people. Such meetings are a means to:

• Pass along information. Higher-level managers and supervisors need information in order to make good decisions. They can and should get it from their people because workers closest to the job often have better knowledge of problems in getting out the work.

• Bring the employee and the company closer together. Meetings improve loyalty. They are also a way of giving recognition to individuals and developing a better group and team spirit.

• Enhance the status of first-line managers by making them look capable in the eyes of the workers. In addition, a meeting can make managers more alert to people's needs and problems.

• Provide training for other jobs. Meetings are a way to let department members know what others in the department are doing. They also broaden people's knowledge about the quality and quantity of the company's product or service and the company's customers.

Explaining Your Decisions

Every time you make a decision involving your people, you face a related problem: Should you explain the decision before you make it, after you've made it, or not at all? If you think about this problem, you will probably realize that it's a good idea to make sure your people understand the reasons for your decisions, and the most effective time to explain a decision is before you make it.

There are three benefits to getting your people involved before you decide anything. First, you're bound to get more cooperation because you're communicating your confidence in your subordinates' knowledge, abilities, and skills. Second, increased productivity will likely result because any disagreements can be identified and dealt with before the decision is implemented. And third, teamwork should improve because you've started the ball rolling in that direction.

Several good things happen when you include with each decision an explanation of why you decided the way you did:

• You can explain your thinking before anyone can object. Thus, you have a chance to sell your decision. You put any resisters in a position where they have to fight your decision, discount your reasons, and offer alternatives.

• You can avoid sounding defensive by expressing yourself positively, and you enable your supporters to get busy and help sell your decision. If you waited to answer your critics or remained silent, you would lose the opportunity to get early acceptance of your decision.

• You give your people a chance to learn how you make decisions. Subordinates are usually excellent students. They study every move their boss makes. In addition, your people need to know what is important to you.

• You can emphasize critical points in a decision. Your people will learn to give you the facts you need to make good decisions, and with a little practice, they will be able to anticipate your decisions.

What happens if you don't explain your decisions? You risk developing a lot of undesirable attitudes, beliefs, and behaviors in your people, such as suspicion, hostility, lack of confidence, and mistakes. Worst of all, you lose an opportunity to gain participation and input from them.

Chapter Six

Analysis Procedures

Science is becoming more and more important in the development of objective decision-making methods, which can be ranked by how much they involve theory and scientific procedure. The totally objective, scientific approach to decision making is at one end of such a ranking, while the approach involving intuition, experience, and subjective application of knowledge is at the other. A mixture of the two extremes is generally used to solve most problems. Yet the subjective approach has been the basis for much decision making in the past. A supervisor can seldom explain in depth the basis for his or her hunches but can do remarkably well with them regardless.

More first-line managers are relying today on mathematics in making decisions. They are finding that matrixes are convenient methods for representing logical statements and depicting systems. Many of today's managers are deeply involved in or highly dependent on information processing and retrieval. The computer has played an important role in this respect and will contribute heavily in the future. In addition, word processing has enabled all levels of management to more clearly and quickly document and implement decisions of all types.

Several special information sources help problem solvers and decision makers. Accounting contributes information by way of financial statements and cost and performance reports. If these are understood by supervisors and reach them promptly, the principle of exceptions can be applied, resulting in better decisions. The statistician provides certain nonaccounting data, designs sampling studies and interprets their findings, creates operations research tools, and formulates statistical decision rules for management use. Computers provide greatly increased amounts of data much faster than ever before; they thus become optimally useful in helping people make good decisions.

The decision maker's reliance on science varies according to the management level of the decision. Scientific procedures are most applicable to lower-level decision making, although the use of the scientific method encompasses all levels of management. In recent years, it has begun to indirectly affect upper-level decision making. As the validity of using scientific decision methods to solve problems has become apparent, managers have provided support and encouragement for these methods. Still, decision theory is felt to be in its infancy. The new methods not only solve existing problems in new ways but also change the nature of those existing problems.

Mathematical Techniques and Tools

To use mathematics as a decision tool, you must understand it as a language. Since it differs from other languages, the first step in applying it to an office or factory problem is to translate the description of the problem function from its familiar vocabulary into the language of mathematics. To do this, you must generalize, identify, and quantify your goals as well as your limitations or restrictions. You can get data from your cost and accounting departments, but this is ordinarily not enough. You need to supplement it with estimates and approximations of the function that you are concerned with. As a first-line manager, expect that you will need the help of your staff and data processing people when you use mathematics as a decision tool.

A common misunderstanding about the language of mathematics is the belief that precise numerical statements require equal precision factually. Mathematics can be an effective decision-making tool even in circumstances in which the values assigned to costs are no more than approximations. Looking at mathematics in this light, the mathematical approach is more precise and consistent, and therefore more rational, than judgment based on intuition and experience.

A way of using mathematics in making decisions is to consider the probabilities of something undesirable happening. For example, a company that wants to reduce the risk of a machine breakdown may determine the probability that a component of the machine will fail after it has been operated a given period of time. This can be done by figuring that after 6 months, the chance of failure may be 20 percent; after 12 months, 40 percent; and so on. The company can then replace the component when the chance of failure reaches 50 percent. Use of this technique is possible, of course, only when the company has enough history on the performance of the machine to calculate the odds with some degree of accuracy.

In mathematical decision making, a supervisor must sometimes make a distinction between risk and uncertainty, risk being the case where the probabilities are known or can be estimated by the use of good judgment and uncertainty being the case where the supervisor has absolutely no way of judging the odds. Although mathematical techniques do not always make the decision for a supervisor, they do furnish systematic ways of presenting the possible results when he or she faces a problem in which many of the factors that will affect the outcome are beyond his or her control.

Quantifiable Factors

Another form of mathematical decision making concerns quantifying the factors bearing on the problem. To illustrate this process, consider the purchase of new equipment by a company, not to take care of increased demand for its output but to save on labor costs. If a machine priced at $20,000 will reduce annual costs for a process or operation by $10,000, it will pay for itself in two years, and if no other factors are involved, it will be a better choice than a machine with a payoff period of four years. Or if the costs of maintaining an old machine are higher than the depreciation on a new one, it will be cheaper to make the purchase.

Of course, there are other factors that may influence calculations of this nature, and even though a first-line manager may not be involved, he or she should be knowledgeable of them. For example, many companies take the time value of money into account in making capital investments. They calculate the return that could be expected if the money were put to other uses. They also weigh the cost of delay and the expense of gathering more information against the risk of proceeding with what they already have, which may well be incomplete.

A few assumptions must be made with this type of reasoning. One is that the market for the product made (the equipment output) will remain constant or grow. If the demand were to drop, the labor need would also drop, and the figures used in the calculations would change. Another assumption is that the product will not change enough in the future to make it possible to eliminate the operation entirely. A third assumption is that the best new machine now on the market is the ultimate, at least for a few years; thus, it will not be replaced by something else within a year or two, in which case it might be better to wait.

Unquantifiable Factors

Supervisors are sometimes required to make decisions where it is not possible to quantify the pertinent factors. In a few cases, it may not even be possible to judge later whether their choices were the best possible. This means that they must rely heavily on their hunches or intuition.

A hunch has been described earlier as a feeling that something is going to happen in a certain way and that, therefore, a certain action would likely be good or bad. The hunch may be completely unsupported, or it may be close to a reasonable judgment. For instance, a first-line manager may be able to predict with some degree of accuracy the reaction of his or her people to an edict that management is going to issue. A hunch of this type may be quite accurate because the person having it senses it as representing a good cross section of other people's feelings and opinions. The safety sense an experienced and long-time construction supervisor is said to possess or a good job trainer's hunch about how quickly some workers will learn a new job may be due to this factor. Hunches, of course, may be entirely inaccurate. They may be based on wishful thinking or on subconscious associations that have no relevance to the situation.

Judgment is often difficult to define, in that reasoning can never produce a conclusion that is assuredly the best. The case for one alternative rather than another can never be proved beyond a shadow of a doubt, as can a theorem in geometry. Good judgment may be looked upon as a human quality that is inborn yet can be greatly improved through long experience. It may be said that some first-line managers have naturally good business judgment, but only after they have experienced many different business situations can such judgment reach its full potential.

Many executives who are accustomed to making numerous decisions in the course of a day do not know how they make them. Even company presidents have made such remarks as, "You don't know how you do it—you just do it," and "That's like asking a professional golfer to explain the swing that has always come naturally to him or her."

The steps preparatory to making decisions are easier to identify and define than the procedure itself. For supervisors, these include assessing people's capabilities; the availability of material; and the various contingencies of time, past practice, and cost, among others. In some cases, decisions are a matter of compromise, particularly if a management/union contract is in effect or the company is in an austerity period and supervisors are under pressure to reduce costs. For example, a decision about whether or not to work people overtime is frequently made by a first-line manager. Top management tends to question his or her judgment only if shipments to customers are delayed or services are not provided on schedule.

Decision-Making Tools

When you are given a particular problem and have several techniques you can use to arrive at a solution, which technique can be expected to produce the best results? To answer this question, you must consider three factors: feasibility, reliability, and cost. Although there are other factors you might consider, they will not influence most supervisory decisions.

The feasibility of a technique is usually easy to determine. If no computer were available to a problem solver, it would not be feasible for him or her to go to the trouble of borrowing or renting one for the sole purpose of solving a particular problem. It would also not be feasible to attempt to solve a complex simulation problem without a computer.

The major factor that must be considered in selecting a decision-making tool is its level of reliability. How much error in a particular solution is tolerable? In arriving at a solution, you would like to know not only the estimated payoff but how reliable that estimate is. Some tools are highly reliable—you can be reasonably certain that the values of the estimated and actual solutions will be almost the same.

When the reliability of a decision tool is known, risk or uncertainty is less. You may be willing to accept a solution with less payoff if it has greater reliability. But when you reach a decision intuitively, reliability can seldom be determined ahead of results because it is very difficult to test a solution that you reached unsystematically. Although a solution may initially seem to have merit, it may produce results that are significantly different from what you expected. The person who makes a decision intuitively cannot be sure within a predictable range that the expected payoff will actually happen.

As with any venture, the cost of the procedure or tool is a determinant of whether you use it or some other method. To determine the total cost of taking a mathematical or analytical approach to a problem, you should consider the time, the cost of staff people, and the cost of use of the computer. The pay rate of programmers and the cost of computer time are not difficult to figure, but the total time for a particular technique could vary considerably, depending on such factors as the availability of data and the number of variables. The cost of data collection can be significant in problem solving.

Decision-making tools generally are operational only when certain conditions exist. Futhermore, various limitations can restrict their use. Several illustrations of these drawbacks can be given. Functions must be linear if linear programming is to be used. The model with which you work in simulation must reasonably reflect the reality you are trying to understand or control. In fact, the use of all models has some drawbacks.

Most models are theoretical and impersonal, and some are

very difficult to understand. A mathematical model may require oversimplification in order to be manipulated. Then again, there is no guarantee that the time spent in constructing the model will pay off in good prediction. The symbolic language may also be a problem. Even a mathematician may have difficulty in managing the model so as to obtain useful results. In gambling-game problems, it may be easier to play a large number of games and determine the probabilities directly than to attempt a mathematical analysis of the probabilities.

If a preliminary survey of the problem reveals that the conditions necessary for effective use of special techniques do not exist, these tools should not be considered. You may also have a constraint in that if a solution to a problem is needed in a few days, the techniques that require more time cannot be used. Another serious constraint may be a shortage of trained personnel to assist you. Some techniques are highly sophisticated. If people trained in such techniques are lacking, your method of analysis would have to be restricted to the skills of the available staff. A final constraint may be that you have an excessive number of problems to solve. Your boss may decide that you should turn to procedures that will conserve managerial time.

Statistical Analysis

Statistics can contribute to more effective decision making in a number of ways. First, the statistician provides certain of the quantitative data that management requires but that accounting does not provide. The statistician also designs sampling surveys, market research, and other experiments such that maximum information will be provided from a study and then helps to interpret the findings correctly and logically when the studies are completed. In addition, the statistician helps in formulating useful decision rules and creates new tools for operations research.

Suppose someone hands you a group of figures. The figures could be a record of nearly any activity in the company, such as production tonnage, machine failures, or some other incidents. Of what value are the figures in helping you to make a decision? The figures don't mean much unless they are analyzed, a procedure that is called statistical analysis. By statistical analysis you determine the relationship of each number to all the others. With this knowledge, you are able to make decisions. But that's a very simple explanation. In actuality, statistical analysis takes place in several steps: compiling the figures or data, organizing and analyzing them, evaluating conclusions, searching for cause-and-effect relationships, and detecting trends.

Marginal and Cost-Benefit Analysis

Decision makers sometimes need to call upon specific analysis procedures when faced with making a difficult decision. Such a situation may arise in the evaluation of alternatives. Although marginal analysis is commonly used in accounting, it can also be used in comparing factors other than costs and income. For example, to determine the optimum output of a process line or a machine, you vary input against output until the additional input equals the additional output. This would then be the maximum efficiency point. Another example—closer to home, perhaps—is the study that your boss makes in deciding how many people should report to you. He or she may increase the number to the point where incremental savings in costs, better communication, and other factors equal incremental losses in your effectiveness in carrying out the responsibilities of your position.

Cost-benefit analysis is another technique used in evaluating alternatives. The procedure enables weighing alternatives where the optimum cannot be measured in dollars or some other specific unit. However, it is not necessary that objectives be capable of being measured specifically. For example, if a first-line manager implemented a program for improving employee morale, the program's effectiveness may be measured by such verifiable factors as the number of grievances submitted, the percentage of absenteeism, and the labor turnover.

The following characteristics of cost-benefit analysis distinguish it from other methods of analysis:

- Objectives are normally end results and are usually imprecise.

- Alternatives customarily include programs and procedures for reaching objectives.
- Cost estimates may include nonmonetary as well as monetary costs.

Cost-benefit analysis can be enhanced by using models and other operations research techniques. Cost models can be developed to show the cost of each alternative. Similarly, effectiveness models can be constructed to show the relationship between each alternative and its effectiveness. Models that combine these two can then be made to show the relationships between costs and effectiveness for each alternative. Cost-benefit analysis thus enables decision makers to evaluate various alternatives as to their effectiveness versus their costs.

Operations Research

Operations research is defined as the application of mathematical methods to the study and analysis of complex problems. The techniques for solving problems using operations research methods include simulation, queuing, linear programming, and others. Typical problems that can be solved are determining the optimum time for performing preventive maintenance, the optimum number of people who should be employed in a storeroom for minimum cost, and the lowest level of machine parts inventory that should be maintained consistent with management policy. Many problems can be handled by the computer by constructing models simulating actual conditions in the office, factory, warehouse, or storeroom and then studying the effect of altering the variables.

Decision-Making Models

A decision-making model is a representation that shows how decisions should be made. The effectiveness of a decision is in large part determined by the particular decision model used. Problem solvers continually seek a good model, one that will provide the greatest number of solutions with a high output per solution at the least cost over a specific time period. The measure of the output of a decision is defined as the extent or degree to which the decision aids in reaching the company's objectives. Effective models assure an integration of managerial activities so that efforts are directed toward a common purpose. They also provide an order that will bring about consistent, predictable behavior.

The use of a model is illustrated by the determination of the economic order quantity (EOQ) of a storeroom item that the company purchasing agent might order. The variables involved are the ordering cost in dollars, the annual usage in units, the inventory carrying cost, and the unit cost of the item in dollars. The model, expressed in equation form, is:

$$EOQ = \sqrt{\frac{2AS}{IC}}$$

where A = ordering cost in dollars
S = annual usage in units
I = inventory carrying cost as a decimal
C = unit cost of the item in dollars

To illustrate the use of the formula, you can work it out for an item that, based on the storeroom records, costs $50 each and of which the plant uses about 75 a year. The cost of issuing a purchase order is about $65, and the inventory carrying cost is about 30 percent of the value of the storeroom inventory, or .30 in decimal form. Therefore:

$$EOQ = \sqrt{\frac{2 \times 65 \times 75}{.30 \times 50}} = \sqrt{650} = 25.5$$

The quantity that should be ordered by the purchasing agent is 26. The theory behind economic order quantity buying is that the cost of carrying inventory and the cost of buying are like balance scales—when one goes up, the other goes down.

Simulation

The use of a model to simulate a condition or situation is a very effective tool for a manager concerned with planning and control. Today, the technique of simulation through use of mathematical models and the computer enables you to construct a model of a problem and test the results of any number of proposed courses of action. Even with its limitations, the procedure may provide unanticipated information and thus enable you to avoid making a poor decision.

Simulation need not be mathematical, but many of today's business problems are so complex and the important variables so numerous that mathematics and the help of the computer are needed. Some examples of areas of responsibility where simulation is of value are those involving inventory control and the procedures required to operate a new process or production line. Although a supervisor may feel uncertain about how to proceed, simulation of a course of action can at least give him or her some indication of the size and type of risks involved.

Queues (Waiting Lines)

Another mathematical technique based on operations research theory has been derived for solving waiting-line problems. A user of this technique balances the costs of waiting lines versus the costs of preventing them by providing increased service. The theory is based on the premise that although delays may be expensive in one or more ways, eliminating them may be even more costly.

The people waiting in line at a storeroom window in an industrial plant are a good example of this problem. When a machine breaks down on the production line and can be repaired by use of a part or component in the storeroom, both production time and repair labor time are lost if the mechanic has to wait to be taken care of. But how often does a mechanic have to stand in line? Can adding another storeroom clerk to the payroll be justified?

A similar problem concerns the unloading of tank cars, boxcars, and delivery trucks. Although a company wants to avoid paying demurrage charges and quickly get materials into the warehouse, it may not be able to keep an additional employee busy on such operations. Rather than hire someone who may be idle part of the time, the company should first make a waiting-line study of the existing arrival and delivery situation, along with the time it takes to complete the unloading operations. The study will reveal whether or not an additional person on the payroll would save the company money.

Linear Programming

For one of the most successful applications of operations research in problem solving, look to the technique called linear programming. It is based on the assumption that a linear, or straight-line, relationship exists between variables and that the limits of variations can be determined.

The production line in a plant is a good candidate for application of the technique by a first-line manager. The major variables in this case are the units produced per machine in a given time, material costs per unit, direct labor costs, and machine operating costs. Most or all of these variables have linear relationships within certain limits; by solving linear equations that express those relationships, you can learn the optimum conditions of costs, machine use, time periods, and other objectives of the production department. This problem-solving procedure is especially useful where input data can be quantified and the progress toward objectives can be measured.

Linear programming is appropriate for solving problems of production planning, use of warehouse and storage areas to permit extended production runs to hold those costs to a minimum, and routing of shipments to take advantage of low shipping rates. The major drawback to the use of the technique today is that it depends on linear relationships between variables. If relationships are not linear, the technique cannot be used.

The Limitations of Operations Research

Although operations research has great potential for solving many types of different problems, it does have some limitations. It is not the answer to every business problem, nor is it a source of automatic decisions. It is limited to the study of tangible, measurable factors. The many factors affecting business decisions that remain intangible or qualitative must continue to be evaluated by judgment and intuition. The experts in applying operations research theory point out this distinction between the operations research responsibility for analysis and the executive responsibility for decisions.

Operations research has been used only sparingly in solving supervisory and higher-level managerial problems. A difficulty with the technique is that the number of variables and how they relate to one another require use of higher mathematics, a level beyond the comprehension of most managerial personnel.

In addition, although probabilities and approximations can be substituted for unknown quantities, many important managerial decisions involve qualitative factors. Until such factors can be quantified, operations research applications will be limited, and the selection of alternatives will continue to be based on judgments that are not quantitative.

Another problem with operations research lies with how the supervisor or higher-level manager relates to the trained operations researcher. First-line managers in general lack a knowledge and understanding of mathematics, just as mathematicians generally are not knowledgeable about managerial problems. Although curriculums at universities and business schools have started to deal with this problem, it remains a major reason why operations research has not been fully accepted as an important aid in decision making.

Risk Analysis and Risk Preference

Several other techniques for analyzing problems are available to help supervisors in making decisions. Two techniques—risk analysis and risk preference—involve the risk associated with the act.

Decision makers dealing with uncertainty like to know how much risk they are taking when determining what course to follow. The operations research technique does not provide such information because many of the inputs to the model are merely estimates, while others are based on probabilities. Managerial personnel are customarily aided by estimates prepared by staff members, but the risk element is not covered under this procedure.

The decisions that a first-line manager must make in planning and carrying out a project are based on the relationships between several variables, many of which contain some uncertainty coupled with a fairly high degree of probability. Thus, the wisdom of undertaking a project might depend on the individual costs of labor, equipment, and material. A best estimate of the total cost might thus be made.

But suppose that further study of each of the three variables shows that the labor cost has an 80 percent probability of being accurate, the equipment cost estimate a 90 percent chance of being correct, and the material cost estimate a 70 percent probability of being correct. In this case, the calculated probability of the total cost estimate for the entire project's being right would almost certainly be less than 85 percent; exactly how much less would depend upon the values of each variable. However, the probability of all the estimates of the three variables' being correct is only 50.4 percent (.80 × .90 × .70).

The risk-analysis technique involves the preparation of a probability distribution curve for each variable. This is done by gauging the range and probability of each variable. No matter how judgmental the preparer of these estimates may be, a range of values and probabilities is better than a single best estimate. Given such information as this, a supervisor is better able to determine the probability of completing a project within a specified maximum cost.

When statistical probabilities are used in making decisions, personal judgment must still be relied upon. It would seem likely that if you had a 70 percent chance of a decision's being the right one, you would take it. But this is not necessarily true, since the risk of being wrong is 30 percent. You might not want to take this risk, particularly if the consequences of being wrong are serious, whether in terms of reputation, job security, or monetary loss.

In order to treat probabilities in a practical manner in decision making, you need to look at how you face risk and how much risk you are willing to take. This varies among decision makers according to the amount of risk involved and whether or not it is thought the company can afford a loss. Higher-level managers are accustomed to taking greater risks than first-line managers; their types of decisions involve more risk. A higher-level manager may be instrumental in changing company policy or operating procedure, while a first-level supervisor may not take any risk greater than promoting low-skilled workers or approving their vacations.

It must be remembered, too, that a manager who may make a decision involving thousands of dollars for his or her company on a given project with a chance of success of perhaps 70 percent would not be likely to do that with his or her own money, at least not unless he or she were quite wealthy. Also, the manager who is willing to take a 70 percent risk in one case might not be willing in another. How a person feels about taking a risk varies with activities, events, people, and positions, not to mention the person's mood at the moment.

Some people avoid risks in certain situations and act like gamblers in others. Some people are by nature risk takers, and others are overly cautious in everything they do. Risk preference can be illustrated in a series of curves, as shown in Figure 1. This series shows the risk avoider's curve, the gambler's curve, and the average person's curve. The latter curve indicates that most of us are gamblers when the risk is low but become avoiders when the risk increases.

Many higher-level managers and probably most supervisors are risk avoiders because they are very much aware of the dangers of failure. Since they do not "play the averages," it can be concluded that statistical probabilities are not appropriate for making many of their decisions.

The Computer's Influence

Computer-aided decision making is no longer the exclusive province of the theoretician and the mathematician. It is an operating tool that is available to help managers at all levels in an organization run their operations. Complex and sophisticated programming systems and software that operate on computers of every size are available as complete packages that require little if any modification to run effectively in the user's environment. With a wide selection of systems available for large and small computers, management no longer has to consider making the extensive in-

Figure 1. Risk preference illustrated.

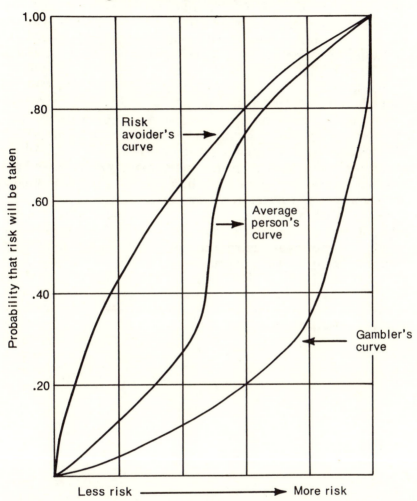

house programming investment that once was mandatory. But this is not to say that a company deep into use of the computer does not need a programming staff. User departments continually find new applications for the computer; if the application is new or unique to the company, programmers are essential.

There is little question that the much-discussed and well-publicized concept of the office of the future and the automated plant have become realities. Clerical staff, secretaries, line and staff, and administrative personnel are more likely today to touch the keys of a word processor or personal computer than those of a typewriter or calculator. U.S. Commerce Department statistics have shown that managers and executives can increase their productivity up to 25 percent with the installation and use of properly automated work stations.

Computers and data processing systems have helped many first-line managers in making decisions. When all the data and information have been programmed into a computer, it can make minor decisions. Most problems facing managers, however, are not that simple. The computer is best used as a supplier of data and information, which a supervisor uses to arrive at a decision. Computers enable higher-level managers and supervisors to make decisions faster because the data are available to them more rapidly. Computers also provide the means for a deeper analysis of complex situations. By using mathematical models, the computer can simulate problem situations and project the results from different courses of action. It is a fact that computers and data processing have helped greatly to make decision making an easier and less stressful activity.

Chapter Seven

Making a Choice

All people make decisions that affect their own actions. First-line managers are chiefly concerned with making decisions that will influence the actions of others. The decision-making process of management is thus affected by the environment of the decision maker and the role he or she assumes. The result of the process is a decision that can be defined as a course of action consciously chosen from known alternatives for the purpose of achieving an objective.

Note that three important points are made with this definition. First, a decision involves a choice; if there is only one alternative, no decision is possible. Second, a decision involves mental activity at the conscious level; the logical aspects are important, but emotional, nonrational, and subconscious factors may influence the process. Third, a decision is made for a purpose; an objective lies behind every decision.

Premises

The search for and analysis of alternatives and their probable consequences is the decision-making step most subject to logical and systematic treatment. The logical approach is the key to this step. Logic involves the way in which the mind goes from a premise (a statement of the relationship between a cause and a consequence) to propositions based on the premise.

Use of the premise principle has long been considered a way of imagining in detail what the results of choosing an alternative would be. The objective in making a decision is to choose from among the various alternatives the one or ones that will result in the largest number of wanted consequences and the smallest number of unwanted consequences. In order to determine which is best, you can test each alternative in turn by imagining that each (but not the others) has already been put into effect and then trying to foresee in detail what the probable desirable and undesirable consequences of adopting that alternative would be. When you've done this, you are in a position to compare the alternatives.

The statements of wanted and unwanted consequences are what are called premises. All of us use premises in making decisions, even though we may not be aware of them. We don't mention them or attempt to describe them if we are alone. But when several people discuss a problem and try to make a decision, each one tries to list the consequences he or she foresees. Essentially, what decision makers are saying is that if one alternative or another is put into effect, they would expect certain results to follow, some of which are desirable and some undesirable.

Just about every alternative we consider will produce both wanted and unwanted consequences. We should be skeptical of an alternative that seems to be either completely out of the question or the perfect answer. We should take a second look at any such proposal because the chances are that we have made up our minds too soon, having decided to accept or reject it before considering the consequences. Sometimes we are so impressed with an alternative we have discovered that we unconsciously build up its benefits and shut out of our minds the negative results we do not want to see.

You can also define a premise as a statement containing a description of both a cause and a result that applies to the alternative you are considering. Thus, your premise on a change you might make in the office could be presented as, "If I approve the purchase of a word processor" (the cause), "the morale of the secretaries in the department will rise" (the result).

Although the reliability of the premises a person takes into consideration has a great deal to do with the outcome of the decision made, the soundness of the person's prediction of outcome has nothing to do with whether the person uses it as a premise. Of course, no one uses a premise that he or she thinks is unreliable—it is automatically discarded. People keep and use only those premises they believe will turn out to be true, only those describing results they actually expect to occur.

Supervisors must consider the effect of their decisions on their people. For instance, adopting a "no overtime" policy with employees who have been accustomed to working it on a regular basis will probably be viewed by them as cutting their pay. Some of them will naturally object, since it will result in a lowering of their standard of living. While the supervisor in this case may have no alternative, he or she should at least prepare people for this change instead of springing it on them suddenly.

Ordinarily, the more premises you take into consideration, the better your decision will be, provided that you also meet certain conditions. You should be considering the most promising alternatives; the premises used for each should be reasonably reliable; the most significant ones should have been considered; and the premises should have been given appropriate weights. When you foresee that the rightness or wrongness of a decision will have an effect on your own welfare or on that of your company, this extra effort in making the decision is well worthwhile. Most of us tend to make decisions without sufficient forethought and, as a result, may be disappointed when we carry them out and see the consequences.

One of the main reasons why our decisions occasionally look unwise when viewed in retrospect is that one or more of the premises we used were unreliable—our predictions of the consequences proved to be wrong. We see that we jumped to the conclusion that certain things would happen in response to a given cause. In making an important decision, you must recheck the reliability of at least the more important premises, the ones that will have the greatest impact on the department and the company.

The concept of premises may be carried further by thinking of the cause and the result as being predominately factual or predominately value. A factual element is one that is measured objectively, and a value element is one that is measured subjectively. The higher a person's position on the company hierarchy ladder, the more value premises the person must consider. For those at the bottom of the ladder, workers in the factory and clerks in the office, the majority of the premises needed in making their decisions are factual. Workers, for example, use premises about how machines and equipment will operate and how the workers must move their hands, not only for convenience, but also for efficiency. Many of the causes and results are tangible. Frequently, the decisions made by their first-line managers are also based primarily on predictions of what machines will do and the consequences of hand movements. But the managers must also use some value premises. For instance, a first-line manager, in deciding who to put on a difficult repair job, must consider the skills and qualifications of the available craftspersons for that job and also how well each would like the job. If the manager knows his or her people well, such a decision is relatively easy.

Some supervisors never learn how to handle value premises. A supervisor who feels insecure in using them and therefore relies mainly on factual premises for fear his or her recommendations will prove wrong frequently makes bad decisions—ones that are quite wrong. To such a person, value premises seem to have no general pattern and seem to be mixed-up and inconsistent. Consequently, the supervisor is always looking for formulas, keys, and principles that will clarify matters. But even after finding these tools, he or she is unable to apply them to a particular problem. To add to the person's difficulties, the principles are usually so fragmentary that he or she can seldom find one to fit the problem at hand. Supervisors who apply operations research principles for solving problems and include only selected factual premises in reaching their tentative decisions occasionally encounter trouble in making good decisions.

People who have been schooled to work with factual premises are often out of their element when using value premises. For instance, engineers, physicists, chemists, mathematicians, and statisticians, trained to use facts and figures and exclude all other factors, usually do not become managers and executives until after they have demonstrated that they can use value premises with confidence and assurance. An inexperienced person with scientific training often fails as an executive because to him or her, value premises are no good; they are emotional; they cannot be put into an equation as independent or dependent variables, nor are they trustworthy.

Considering Alternatives

When you have a clear objective and must make a decision to reach that objective, your next step is to consider the alternatives. Seldom do you find that you have no alternatives. In fact, if it appears that you have only one course to follow, there's a good chance that it's wrong. In such a case, you probably have not forced yourself to consider other ways. This is necessary if your decision is to be the best one possible under the circumstances.

The ability to develop and consider alternatives is often as important as choosing the best one. Yet ingenuity, research, and innovation may uncover so many choices that you can't properly evaluate every one. Your best bet in this situation is to limit your search for alternatives to those that answer or satisfy a requisite of your decision.

A requisite is defined as a condition that your decision must meet if the decision is to accomplish your objective. The common definition of a requisite is: that which is essential or necessary. If you clearly recognize a requisite, you should confine your search for alternatives to those that will meet it. The better you are able to do this, the better job you will do in selecting the best course to follow.

Recognizing a requisite is not always easy. For example, if a first-line manager were looking for ways to increase production, one of the factors that must be contended with might be that management will not hire more people. The attitude of the present employees toward working overtime could also be a factor. Looking for and recognizing requisites in planning never ends. For one project at one time, a certain requisite may be critical to the decision; but at a a later date and for a similar decision, the requisite may be something else. A supervisor may have been given the authority to acquire new equipment when the requisite was availability of money, only to have the requisite become delivery.

The Problems of Evaluation

Most decision makers periodically encounter difficulties in selecting the best alternative. Although the difficulties vary from one situation to another, none is really insurmountable; many problems may be resolved in more than one way. When two or more alternatives seem equally satisfactory, the best thing to do to settle the issue is to toss a coin. If both or all will work equally well, why worry? When it appears that no single alternative will provide the entire answer, use the two or three best alternatives simultaneously. Don't feel that because you use one alternative you cannot use another.

Another problem you may sometimes face is that the unwanted causes and consequences appear so large, unpleasant, or disagreeable that they upset you—you hesitate and don't want to go ahead. If you rank the premises, you will usually feel better about the situation; one or two premises leading to a decision to accept an alternative may be of such a great consequence that they will offset a large number of unwanted effects.

Organizing the premises into separate groups often helps to overcome the difficulty of confusion resulting from having too many of them. This procedure also helps you to uncover premises that you would otherwise have overlooked, especially the unwanted consequences. Sometimes it happens that none of the alternatives you've considered will prove satisfactory. After studying them, you realize that they will all result in too many undesirable effects. Or you see that none of the alternatives is good enough to give you the results you want or achieve the goals you have in mind. In these cases, you have a real problem. You must either go through the process of creating or finding a new alternative or revise the most promising alternative of those you've considered.

Once you have recognized the alternatives, the next step is to evaluate them and select the one that will best enable you to reach your objective. While you may be inclined to favor the alternatives that are quantitative (the consequences of their adoption can be measured), you risk making a bad decision if you ignore those that are qualitative (intangible in nature). There have been numerous cases in industry where management's quantitative plans were voided by an unexpected sitdown or strike, or a new equipment installation didn't solve a problem because of a government agency regulation. These examples show the importance of giving equal attention to quantitative and qualitative factors in the comparison of alternatives.

To evaluate an intangible factor, you must first recognize it and then determine whether you can measure or approximate what its effect might be. If you cannot measure it, learn as much as possible about it to determine its importance. This will enable you to give the factor the weight you feel it deserves. Although such a procedure involves your personal judgment, few business decisions can be so accurately quantified that judgment isn't necessary. Supervisory decision making isn't that simple. Even a successful top-level executive has been described as a person who guesses right.

Selecting Alternatives

As we have seen, decision making frequently involves the evaluation of alternatives. The evaluation includes reasoning, the weighing of advantages and disadvantages, and the consideration of consequences. In selecting alternatives, the decision maker can call upon three resources: experience, testing, and research.

Experience serves a decision maker well, although it may not deserve the high rating it is often given. Experienced first-line managers generally feel that what they have accomplished and what they have learned from the mistakes they made on the job furnish them an almost error-proof guide to future decision making. This feeling is likely to be stronger the more experience a manager has.

The belief that experience is the best teacher is justifiable. Managers who have years of experience are usually strong believers in this. It is true that when decision makers think problems out, make decisions based on their conclusions, and follow up to determine whether their decisions were good, they are bound to improve over a period of time. Many people, however, do not learn from their mistakes; thus, there are those who seem never to get better at making decisions.

You should realize that there is a risk in relying entirely on your experience. Most people do not know why they made a mistake. Then, too, your experience may not apply to new conditions or situations. Decisions pertain to events of the future, experience to those of the past. Yet if experience is studied and analyzed rather than accepted without question, and if the reasons for success or failure are discerned from it, experience will serve you well in making many of your decisions.

An easy way to evaluate alternatives is to try them to see what happens. Of course, often it is not possible to do this, particularly when a decision involves a commitment and cannot readily be reversed. But there are many situations where the only way a supervisor can make sure a plan is right is to try the alternatives to see which is best.

Testing an alternative by trying it should not be resorted to until other planning and analyzing techniques have been tried. At least two reasons support this thinking. Testing can be quite expensive in many situations, especially if capital investment is needed or additional personnel must be provided. Then, too, there may be doubt after an alternative has been tried as to what has been learned, since the future may not match the present.

Still, there are many decisions that cannot be made until more information is obtained or a theory is tested. Even recalling a previous similar situation or carrying out a thorough study may not assure a first-line manager of a correct decision. Studies do not answer all questions; therefore, you should expect to do some experimenting when faced with the task of selecting the best alternative.

Research is a very effective technique for selecting alternatives, particularly when major decisions are involved. The procedure requires that a problem be completely understood in order that the relationships between the factors, variables, and premises may be determined. The technique is well suited for the use of the computer to provide guidance in selecting the best alternative.

Solving a problem by research requires that it be broken into its components and the various tangible and intangible factors studied. Study and analysis are usually less costly than testing. Even though solving a problem may take hours of searching for an optimum solution, the total cost will be less than that of testing the various alternatives.

It is common practice in research studies to develop a model simulating the problem. Engineers customarily make drawings and blueprints as well as three-dimensional forms and prototypes when working on a complex problem; scientists may test many samples in the laboratory. Perhaps the most productive as well as economical use of a model is to simulate the factors and variables in mathematical terms and relationships. Being able to conceptualize a problem mathematically is a major step toward solving it. This approach is becoming more and more popular today in the area of managerial decision making.

Policy as an Aid

Ideally, an inventory of managerial solutions to company problems is stored in the memory of operating managers and supervisors; policy and operating manuals, specifications, and department files contain the written policies, procedures, and standards. Thus, over a period of time, an inventory of solutions to problems is accumulated. When a new problem comes up, a solution is found and is added to the files. Each solution remains in effect as long as management believes it to be the optimum one.

Some solutions may date back a number of years. A billing procedure, for example, might be one that originated when the company was founded. The purchasing policy of the company and the procedure for dealing with contractors may both have had their inception many years ago. Even though such decisions may have been reached some time in the past, they remain unchanged and in effect because employees, supervisors, and higher-level managers understand them and follow them. However, if the manuals and files become voluminous, management personnel may have the problem of selecting the most appropriate solution for a particular situation.

Selecting the right answer to a problem under such conditions is an act of judgment. A highly experienced first-line manager might know all the rules and regulations that apply to the department and its operation and might usually be able to do the right thing, but is this procedure true decision making? The decisions relative to the situation had already been made—the manager merely applied the best one. The question is answered by making a distinction between decision making and decision use. If a manager sees his or her job solely as selecting appropriate solutions for a given problem, the manager is not really performing the managerial function because he or she is not coming up with new answers as they are needed.

The Decision Tree

Through the use of a model commonly known as the decision tree, supervisors can analyze problems and reach decisions that are most likely to accomplish an objective. The decision tree groups are known alternatives for the decision at hand and presents them in pictorial form, thus clarifying the problem.

Figure 2 shows a decision tree for a problem on the cost of a construction project. In this example, the first-line manager must decide what to do after discovering that a construction project under way apparently will cost more than budgeted. Note that the decision tree presents all of the alternatives at a glance. The manager can evaluate each of them methodically and thoroughly in order to decide whether to revise the budget, try to meet it as is, or cancel it.

Despite the fact that only a few companies have used decision trees extensively, growing interest in the technique in recent years suggests that it may become more popular with time. Regardless, the technique replaces judgment by focusing on the critical issues of a problem, bringing out the premises often hidden in judgment, and revealing the steps in reasoning by which decisions are made.

Evaluating a Decision's Importance

Since supervisors have so many decisions to make and make them so frequently, they must be capable of judging the importance of any one decision so that they can give it the attention it deserves. Decisions of lesser importance need not be studied and analyzed; some may even be delegated without concern about passing on one's responsibility, so that what may, in effect, be of little importance to a top-level manager may be of great importance to a supervisor.

Figure 2. The decision tree.

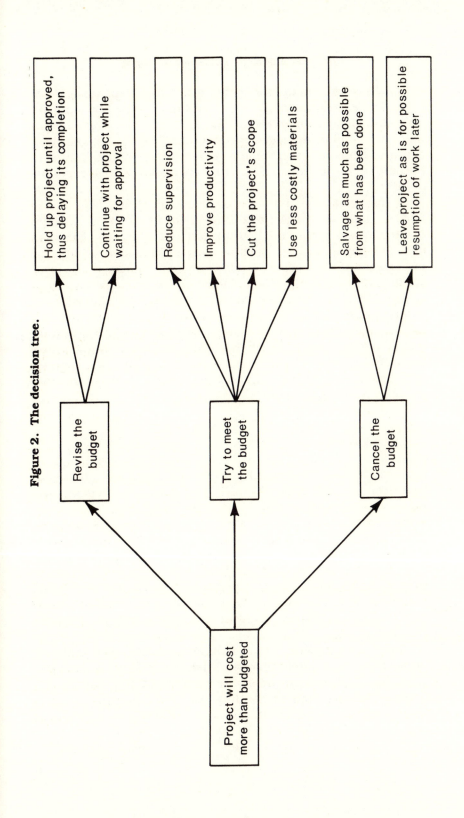

If a decision commits the company to a great expense or to the expenditure of capital money, it should be approved by top management. Most companies specify the maximum commitment that each level of management may make without higher-level approval. Thus, a first-line manager may be very much limited in the amount he or she can spend in carrying out the responsibility of the job.

If goals and objectives of a company are clearly defined and fairly certain, a decision related to them tends to be easier to make than where they are highly uncertain. Where the goals can be accurately quantified, such as with a production facility, the importance of the decision tends to be less than where the goals are difficult to quantify. Most plans of a supervisor can easily be changed, but some may be difficult to change. Decisions of the latter type are more important than those of the former type.

The most important managerial decisions are those that directly concern people. Such decisions are important because people are the source and means of accomplishment, progress, and growth. Any decision that relates to their action or inaction should have their acceptance.

The Best Decisions

After you've made decisions for some time, you'll learn that your best decisions are those that are most objective—that is, ones made without personal and emotional considerations. Consequently, you will try to make more and more decisions that way. Of course, this is easier said than done. A way to go about it is to eliminate all arguments unsupported by facts so that your prejudices aren't in control. One thing that you don't need experience to be aware of concerns taking credit for good results. You should take credit only where you made the decision that produced those results. If you go beyond this, your claims will certainly get you in trouble someday.

If you are inexperienced in making decisions, your boss will know, even more surely than you, that you will make mistakes. When you do, it's better to admit them freely. You may be very nervous, but tell your boss calmly why you made the mistake, what you've learned from it, and what you've done to prevent it from happening again. Since few people are willing to admit their errors, your boss will probably be sympathetic and understanding. Very few managers are fired today for an error honestly made and forthrightly admitted.

You shouldn't worry about making bad decisions—that is, provided you don't make too many and you also learn from them. There are sometimes penalties for making right decisions as well as for making wrong ones. Reprimands may be received for doing nothing or for doing too much. The decision maker who is successful makes decisions objectively and decisively, choosing the right decision calmly from the best alternatives available.

Chapter Eight

Implementing the Decision and Following Up

As you have read, there are many factors to be considered when making a decision. The soundness of your decision depends on whether you have given the proper weight to each of the factors. Before you implement or carry out a decision, it pays to check back over the way you studied and investigated the problem and how you reached your decision. You might ask yourself the following questions:

1. Is the decision compatible with company policy and regulations?
2. Have authorized and interested personnel participated in the decision?
3. Is the decision based on history and experience? Does it deviate from past practice?
4. Does the decision take into account the risk involved and allow for it?
5. Have you considered the timing of your decision? Is it optimum?

6. Is the decision clear and to the point? Does it leave any questions unanswered?
7. If there are several steps to be taken, do you have them in the right order?
8. Will there be any problem in carrying out the decision?
9. Do you expect the decision will be acceptable to those it affects? Must you be prepared to defend it?

If you find that your analysis of the problem and its solution doesn't include some of these factors, reconsider your decision on those matters before you carry it out.

Taking Action

There's a difference between deciding an issue and doing something about it, just as there is a distinction between solving a problem and settling it. That difference is *action.*

Taking action is being decisive. You need action to implement decisions and settle problems. You take action by being forceful, achieving your objective, and standing behind it. All the reasoning, evaluation, and analysis involved in making decisions are as nothing unless they lead to the right conclusion and a prompt execution of it. Action is what counts.

An executive who can't or won't act can actually hold a company back. The problem stems from giving objections, dangers, and risks full weight while assigning short measure to the positive and beneficial arguments. When all the factors and contingencies have been weighed and considered, it is indecisive to feel that more thought is required. Some people would say that this is being too objective, but they would be wrong. Objectivity is understanding. The person who can't or won't act is not suffering from too much objectivity but from too little decisiveness.

Every decision maker wonders: Can I put my decision into effect? Even the top executives of a company feel limited in what they can and cannot do; middle and lower management people are much more limited. Each person is concerned that after determining the right thing to do, he or she might not be able to follow through with it.

Being decisive is really a two-step process. First, you must solve the problem or make the decision. Second, you must sell the solution or implement the decision. There's no getting around the issue. Although some executives may delegate the implementation to a subordinate, it is action that pays off.

Decision makers can best handle the problem of implementation by keeping it in mind from the beginning. In other words, your decision should take into account its implementation as you go through the process of making it. Even though putting a decision into effect is the last step, it is impractical to go through the procedure if you might come up with an answer that no one else will buy. Look for what has to be done and how you will do it. The decision maker who always does what must be done is the one who succeeds. People who proclaim why it can't be done will be left in his or her dust.

Acting Without Deciding

More often than we realize, we act without deciding. For example, let's look at the case of an executive who was fed up with his assistant. The assistant had become careless and negligent. He seemed to have lost his original interest in his job and was now only going through the motions. In the last few months, the executive had frequently thought about firing the assistant but had never found enough courage to do so.

One day the assistant neglected to get started on some urgently assigned work; he was seen several times having coffee and talking with the secretaries. The same morning he offended an important customer and then took two hours for lunch. This behavior was just too much for the executive to take. When the assistant came back to the office, the executive told him that his paycheck was being made out and that this was his last day with the company.

Immediately after doing this, the executive found that he was greatly relieved. He also noticed that the assistant was not disturbed and acted as if he had expected the discharge. The executive asked himself why he didn't make the decision to fire the assistant a long time ago. Under the immediate pressure of that one day, he had acted without going through his normal decision-making procedure.

This case illustrates an interesting facet of decision making.

Essentially, a decision is a resolve to take action, and from time to time, situations may arise where the executive takes decisive action without necessarily thinking of the move as a decision. However, such acts obviously are decisions, or rather are prompted by a decision made unconsciously and spontaneously.

It is apparent that in some situations you can decide without consciously making a decision. Just beware of the pitfall of such action—your spontaneous decision can backfire. There are, for example, documented cases where executives have fired subordinates on the spur of a moment's anger or irritation and regretted the act.

Testing a Decision

Although it is not always possible to test a decision to see if it is a good one, supervisors should be on the alert to do this whenever they can. By testing, unforeseen problems can often be uncovered and mistakes can be corrected before the decision is completely implemented. For instance, a procedure change that a company intends to adopt can be tried in one department before it is introduced in others; a production process method can be tested on a small scale before the entire process line is changed over.

The operations research procedure of simulation, in which mathematical data are fed into a computer, enables a first-line manager to test a theory before implementing it. This form of testing is becoming more and more popular in industrial plants. An example of the application is the situation where management must know how many storeroom attendants are needed to dispense material and miscellaneous supplies to the plant's engineering and maintenance employees.

A major benefit of testing is that it prepares management for roadblocks it may encounter in implementing a decision and for how it may be accepted.

Following Up

The final step in the decision-making procedure is an important one. This is the follow-up and evaluation of the decision after it has been put into effect. Its importance stems from its value in measuring the decision maker's performance, not only in terms of how the problem was approached but also in terms of how correct the decision was.

Unfortunately, the pressures and stress of the job hardly give a supervisor sufficient time to make sure his or her decision is correct, let alone enable him or her to evaluate it. But since the ability or skill of making good decisions is one of the basic qualifications of an effective supervisor, time must be found for appraisal in order to perfect the decision-making skill.

A first-line manager cannot learn how to make good decisions from reading how it's done or from taking the advice of fellow managers. The skill is acquired primarily through experience. But experience can be of value only if the manager follows up and evaluates his or her decisions. Although the ability to make good decisions is one hallmark of effective management, it isn't enough. At some point, decision making must be succeeded by some kind of follow-up for best results. Many otherwise capable supervisors fall down at this crucial point. They think clearly, plan well, and decide intelligently. Then they relax, only to be surprised when things do not work out as planned.

Follow-up is an essential part of being an effective first-line manager. It is a quality higher-level managers notice quickly enough in subordinates—whether or not they really follow through or tend to let things ride and hope for the best. Your boss is equally aware of the same quality, or lack of it, in your own efforts.

A sharp supervisor lets people alone to do a job. At the same time, he or she doesn't fade out of the picture. The supervisor stays in touch, and keeps in control, by following progress. On routine jobs, the supervisor may only stop by occasionally to make sure the employee hasn't run into any difficulties. On larger jobs, he or she may ask a subordinate to figure out the best method, then keep in touch on how things are going. But an alert supervisor always knows the score.

In short, an effective first-line manager knows that good plans and decisions by themselves don't assure good results, that the decision that gets followed up is less apt to get fouled up. Follow-through is just as important in management as it is in tennis or golf. It's the all-important link between good intentions and good results.

Feedback

Feedback permits a supervisor to measure how his or her own behavior is seen by others and whether or not he or she can accurately assess the behavior and motivation of another person. It also enables a supervisor to learn whether his or her judgment of events fits what others see. Through such evaluations, it is possible to experiment and try different courses of action in attempting to solve a problem, with the possibility of testing consequences and improving behavior at the moment.

Good decisions depend on feedback. When a first-line manager receives reports, computer printouts, and other communications regarding what is happening, he or she can make sure that a decision was correct. Through feedback, the manager can determine whether there is a need for revision. However, the greatest value of feedback lies in its revealing how well the decision made achieves the objective. Without this knowledge, a decision maker is in the dark as to whether or not he or she has carried out a responsibility.

Supervisors should make a habit of checking on the effects of their decisions. The best way to do this is to talk to the people affected to see how things are going. Supervisors should also become skilled in observation and in reading body language. There will be times when what they see will tell them more than what they hear.

Controlling the Effects of a Decision

It is through feedback that you are able to control the effects of a decision. Control is needed, since even though you may do an excellent job of planning and selecting the best alternative, your decision may not always be properly or completely carried out. Many things can prevent a decision from being perfectly executed, including stubborn or obstinate people who don't agree with the decision and are unwilling to accept it.

To be able to control the effects of decisions, you must be capable of performing three operations or procedures. First, you must be able to measure what happened when the decision was implemented. Second, you must be able to judge whether the decision brought about the desired condition and met your objective. Third, you must be in a position to take corrective action if necessary.

You get feedback from your decisions both immediately and periodically. The quickest response is generated from your manipulation or adjustment of inanimate objects and devices based on mechanical, electrical, thermal, or nuclear principles. Periodic and often unpredictable feedback comes from people. Until the introduction of instrumentation, operations and procedures now performed by instruments and various control devices were handled by human beings. With the advent of automation evolved the substitution of decisions of an immediate nature made by devices for decisions of an instantaneous nature made by human beings. Many operations in business and industry, however, cannot be controlled by instrumentation. First-line managers who keep a close watch on operations and workers during the workday serve as the controllers. People can easily be replaced by instruments or devices when they use their automatic control systems (such as the nervous system and brain and mechanical-electrical communication systems) in making decisions. But people cannot be replaced where the feedback is complex, varied, and not standard.

Reviewing Your Decision

All follow-up steps should include reviewing your decision. Was it a good one or a bad one? The test of a good decision is to determine whether it accomplished what it was expected to do. If, for example, your decision concerned the reduction of waste, soon after you made it the amount of waste generated should have dropped. If not, your decision did not meet the objective set for it—you still have the problem.

Since the many objectives of most operating decisions of a company are attained in varying degrees and there are usually some gains that do not materialize, it is often difficult to evaluate a decision. To determine the quality of your decision, you must look at the bad consequences as well as the good. But since there may be no way to quantitatively measure these, the best thing you can do is measure the degree of your contentment or regret. You must recognize, of course, that such evaluations aren't truly realistic because they are influenced by face-saving, rationalization, and the resigned realization that the decision had to be made, regardless of its outcome.

If you can't objectively assess the value of a decision, how can you determine when conditions for making a decision are favorable or unfavorable? The only answer to this is to examine the quality of your procedure in making the decision or in following a certain course of action. In this way, you may be able to predict whether a given decision is likely to lead to contentment or regret. Successful decision makers assess their decisions in order to learn from them and enable them to continue making good decisions.

You may sometimes wonder if you are making enough good decisions and what a satisfactory performance on your part should be. The experts say that if more than three out of four of your decisions turn out well, you're shooting par for the course. If you're right seven out of eight times, you're exceptional.

When Your Decision Is Not Accepted

Most first-line managers learn early in their careers that not all of their decisions are readily accepted. You, also, will find that to be the case, even after years of experience. People have their own opinions, think differently than you, and at times may know something that you don't. Questions may be asked by your superiors, peers, and subordinates. Expect this to happen and always be prepared to defend your position.

You have nothing to gain and much to lose by becoming emotional when your decision is questioned, regardless of how certain you are of being right. Highly emotional behavior suggests a lack of stability, personal control, and confidence that supervisors must have if they are to be effective on the job.

The proper way to respond if your decision is challenged is to calmly say that you may be wrong, that everyone has a right to his or her opinion, and that you would like to discuss the matter. Then ask why it is felt that your decision is not good, recognizing all the while that you may have made a bad choice.

Perhaps the best way to handle nonacceptance of a decision is to carefully listen to the person who objects to it. Not only will this help you to better understand the objection, but if the person's arguments are weak, he or she may discover this by being allowed to talk freely. In some cases, your decision may be challenged because people do not understand it or why you made it. Communication may be the problem—if they were not told something that concerned them, you must now do that. You'll find that when you explain, they will often be satisfied.

It stands to reason that someone will sometimes have a valid and logical reason for not accepting your decision. When this happens, tell the person that he or she has made a good point and that you will reconsider. Be sure to praise the person for noticing the problem and calling your attention to it. Review and remake the decision as soon as possible. Keep a person who challenges a decision informed on its status, whether or not you make a new one. When you do this, you show that you recognize and value the person's opinion and judgment and that you hope he or she approves what you subsequently decide. If you reverse the decision or make a new one, go out of your way to see that the person is informed of it ahead of other individuals.

When Decisions Go Bad

What do you do when you make a bad decision? Unfortunately, many people don't know how to proceed. Yet you must do something—you can't let matters run their course or remain as they are. There are several positive moves you can make that may get you out of trouble.

First, recognize that you have a bad situation to deal with and that it may not be your fault. Other people, other events may be partially or wholly to blame. Regardless, you have nothing to gain by accepting a poor situation. People who will not change a decision once it is made only make matters worse. You've got to analyze the problem, learn what happened, and try to save what you can.

Try to retrace your planning so you can discover where things went wrong. If you reached your decision through a multistep process, this should be relatively easy to do. When you reach the step that caused the trouble, revise it to go in the right direction.

What about the decision that looks good on paper but when

executed presents a problem? Does this mean your idea is not plausible and should be abandoned? Not at all. You may merely need to change course, perhaps vary the sequence of the steps or replace one of the inadequate ones. When this is done, the decision may look good again and can be executed.

When you can't correct a decision by retracing your steps, you may need to completely revise your thinking. This is the time to look at the alternatives that you discarded in favor of the one that has gone bad. One or more may now serve as a new decision. You learn how good a job of decision making you are doing through the results of your decisions. Thus, it pays to periodically review your recent ones. Sometimes you can learn more from failure than from success.

Resolving a Bad Decision

Everybody makes a bad decision now and then. Even the most experienced and successful first-line managers do it. But people expect something from you after they learn that you made a bad decision. You must not disappoint them. Your credibility, reputation, and prestige are at stake. Although having to reverse or change your decision may be distasteful as well as leave you feeling weak, you must do what you can to correct your mistake.

Astute supervisors handle themselves well in such a situation and don't lose the respect or admiration of their people. You can do it by explaining briefly and simply the reasons behind your decision to the people involved. But don't go too far with this or you risk sounding defensive. Never apologize for a bad decision. If it caused some inconvenience, a short, sincere comment of regret is enough.

A matter to be concerned with is that you don't make another bad decision when correcting the first one. Get some help and advice when you are considering reversing a decision or making a new one. Talk to the person or persons who were originally involved in it to learn whether they feel that a complete reversal would be wise. They may recommend an alternative course to follow. Get an opinion also from someone you consider knowledgeable and experienced but who was not involved. Decide then what would be your best course of action.

Before you act, however, explain to your boss what has happened and what's on your mind. When you do this, you show that you respect his or her advice. You also demonstrate that you consider it important to keep him or her informed.

A Perspective on Decision Making

In recent years, there has been an increased interest in decision making as a process. Perhaps because of greater competitiveness both within and outside organizations, perhaps because of the recognition of psychology as a factor, or perhaps because decisions today hinge on many more factors and uncertainties than they did in the past—whatever the reason, more emphasis is being placed on making good decisions. Some companies now give their executives and managers training in making decisions in the hope that they will be less indecisive as well as make more correct decisions.

Both indecision and the making of bad decisions are less likely to occur because of lack of knowledge of the procedure itself than because of unfamiliarity with the subject or pressures applied by superiors. Higher-level managers and supervisors who know little about a subject or who have meager experience in an area cannot but feel insecure in taking a position on any aspect of it. Therefore, they postpone their decisions as long as they can. They worry that if they plunge ahead in an effort to appear decisive, they are likely to make a bad mistake.

The pressures of superiors operate in a variety of ways to bring on indecision. If first-line managers do not know just how far they can take it on themselves to make decisions, and if at the same time they risk a great deal of blame by overstepping their authority, they will make as few clear-cut decisions as possible. There are three remedies for such situations that can promote an improvement in decision making:

- Give people more training in areas where they make decisions.
- Change the organization's structure in order to give people at lower levels of management more authority.
- Change the attitude of top management, something that can usually be done only by top management itself.

Supervisors may improve their own decision making by guarding against some of the illogical reasons that may be given for favoring or disapproving certain courses of action. Where they must depend on others to supply them data and information, they should learn enough about the subject or project to ask the right questions.

Making decisions is only one of the skills required of today's first-line managers. They must, in addition, have leadership skills, be well versed in all aspects of human relations, and understand as well as practice the principles of good management.

Decisions are effective only when they are successfully carried out. Many factors influence an organization's decisions. The organization must be sound and well structured. Its objectives should be logical and clearly defined. Planning, scheduling, and control functions must be established and be regarded as responsibilities of each member of management. If an organization is to grow, it should progress in the direction of automating its functions, including the making of decisions. When supervisors are relieved of repetitive tasks and work that can be delegated, they are able to give more attention to making decisions.,

Successful first-line managers understand the process of problem solving and the need for being skilled in the art. They use every possible aid available to them to develop their ability and skill in making good decisions because they recognize the importance of those decisions to their subordinates and to their organization.

Index

acting on decisions, 32-33, 165-167
advice, seeking, 22, 25, 173-174
aids to decision making:
  commitment, 87-88
  commitment warnings, 92
  common-sense approach, 101-102
  conflict, 85-86
  experience, 105-107
  foot-in-the-door technique, 91-92
  heuristic reasoning, 98-99
  intuition, 99-101
  logic, 151-152
  planning, 116-117
  quick thinking, 110-114, 117-118
  self-confidence, 13-16
  social and personal constraints, 88-89
alternatives, considering, 155-159
  and consequences, 152
  defining requisites when, 155
  research studies in, 158-159
  role of experience in, 157-158, 159
  and testing, 158

analysis
  computer-aided, 148-150
  cost-benefit, 141-142
  decision-making tools for, 138-140
  marginal, 141
  mathematical techniques for, 135-136
  operations research, 142-146
  quantifying factors in, 136-137
  risk, 146-148
  unquantifiable factors in, 137-138
anticipatory regret, 80-81
assertiveness, 29-30
assement of decisions, 170-171
authority, principles of:
  chain of command, 69-70
  delegation of authority, 71-72
  management by exception, 73-74
  span of control, 70-71
autonomy, 67-68
avoidance, of decision making, 11, 75-78, 118-119

bias, 95-98
bypassing boss, 126-127

chain of command, 69-70
change
  acceptance of, 25
  announcement of, 63
  combatting resistance to, 65-67
  effectiveness in handling, 26-27
  employee reaction to, 62-63
  follow-up on, 64
  getting employees involved in, 65
  and individual values, 67
  and innovative decisions, 26
  making decisions involving, 67-69
  and personal involvement, 25
  preparing employees for, 63-64
  retracting, 68
  solving problems through, 24-26
commitment in decision making, 79, 88-92
commitment entrapment, 90-91
committees, *see* group decision making
common sense approach, 101-102
communication
  bypassing boss and, 126-127
  importance of, 120-122, 132-133
  informal, 124-126
  of information, 122-123
  meetings and, 131-132
  and participative management, 127-131
  verifying successful, 123-124
company policy
  as aid in decision making, 159-160
  compatibility of, with decisions, 164
  consequences of rigid adherence to, 60-61
  as delegation aid, 59

employee attitude toward, 61
  guidelines for good, 60
  limitations of, 60
  manuals, 59-60, 61, 159
  vague, 61
competence, levels of, in organization, 42-43, 71
computers, 135, 148-150
conflict, creative side effects of, 85-86
consensus, *see* group decision making
consultants, 69
cost-benefit analysis, 141-142
cost decisions, 57-58
credibility, personal, 104-105
cybernetics, 120-121

decision(s)
  acting on, 32-33, 165-166
  action as, 166-167
  avoiding, 103
  "chancy," 79-80
  difficult, 4, 78-79
  evaluating, 170-171
  implementation of, 164-167
  innovative, 4, 26
  postponement of, 27-28
  quick, 9, 10
  routine, 3-4
decisions, bad
  admitting to, 15, 68-69
  due to haste, 80
  entrapment into, 89-92
  learning from, 163
  minimizing, 77
  and negative thinking, 46-47
  resolving, 173-174
  and role of self-esteem, 47
  and stress, 77
  understanding causes of, 172-173

decision making
aids to, *see* aids to decision making
developing skill at, 18-19, 29-31, 32-33
fear of, 78-79
hindrances to, *see* hindrances to decision making
human factors in, 48-53
improving, 68-69, 174-175
insight in, 28-29
mathematical techniques in, 134, 142-146
quick, advantages and disadvantages of, 75-78, 80-81
strategy for, 5-6, 9-10, 16-18
techniques for, 138-140
decision trees, 160-161
directions, giving and receiving, 123-124
disloyalty, employee, 86-87

economic order quantity, 143
emotional maturity, 53-55
emotions and decisions making, 8, 11-12, 19, 23, 53, 151
employee(s)
assigning responsibility to, 69
attitudes toward change, 47
effects of decisions on, 153
job satisfaction of, 50
motivation, 49-53
policies handled by, 72-73
employee participation in decision making, *see* participative management
employee-supervisor relationships, 47-48, 53, 54-55, 132-133
environment, organizational, 151
evaluation, of decisions, 167-168, 170-171

experience, and decision making ability, 2, 105-107, 157-158, 159, 162, 164, 168

fact seeking, *see* information search
failures, learning from, 13
fear, of making decisions, 78-79
feedback, 169-170
files, private, 106
follow-up, 167-174
feedback and, 169-170
reviewing decisions in, 170-171
when decision goes bad, 172-174
when decision not accepted, 171-172
"foot-in-the-door" technique, 91-92

goal accomplishment, 26-27
goals, company, *see* company policy
grapevine, 124-126
group decision making, 33-36
advantages and disadvantages of, 34-35
leader in, 36
outside information in, 35
size of group in, 36

help, seeking, 22, 25, 173-174
heuristic reasoning, 98-99
hierarchy, 3, 31, 70, 154
hindrances to decision making:
anticipatory regret, 81
bias, 95-98
commitment as entrapment, 89-91
conflict, 85-86
fear of "catch" or "rub," 79-80
fear of deciding, 78-79

hindrances to decision making *(continued)*

the five worries, 80-84
misdrection, 93-94
procrastination, 75-78, 118-119
rationalization, 84-85
rushing into decision too quickly, 76-77
human factors in decision making, 48-53
hunches
  decisions based on, 99-101
  and reliability, 138-139
  as an unquantifiable factor, 137-138
  when to act on, 33

implementation, of decision, 164-167
information search
  and bias, 95-96
  and communication, 122-123
  distortion of facts in, 93-94
  ending, 94-95
  lack of, 95
insight, role of, in decision making, 28-29
intuitive thinking, *see* hunches

job satisfaction, 67
judgment
  in business, 138
  distortion of, 95
  and problem solving, 159

logic, role of in decision making, 151-152

managers, *see* supervisors
marginal analysis, 141

mathematical techniques, in decision making, 134, 142-146
  see also operations research
memory building, 111

objectives, personal, 48-49
objectivity, and decision making, 49
operations research
  decision-making models in, 142-143
  limitations of, 145-146
  linear programming in, 145
  queues and, 144-145
  simulation in, 143-144, 150, 167
  and supervisory problems, 146
  in university curriculums, 146
organization level at which decisions should be made, 3, 31, 70, 154
organizational chart, 69-70
organizational environment, 151

"package deal," in commitment to decision, 90
Pareto's law, 44
participative management
  acceptance of by managers, 127-128
  attitudes of employees toward, 128-29
  benefits of, 130
  importance of meetings in, 131-132
  problems with, 130-131
personality traits, 48-49
personal objectives, 48-49
personal problems and work, 54
planning, role of, 116-117

policy decisions, *see* company policy
positive thinking, 46-48
postponement, of decision, 27-28
premises
factual, 154-155
reliability of, 152
value, 154
pressure, *see* stress
probabilities, examining, 146-148, 149
problems, types of:
information, 38-39
inventory, 40-41
labor and material allocation, 39
replacement, 40-41
search, 36-37
waiting line, 37-38
problem solving, 20-41
approaches to, 36-41
complications in, 36-41
guidelines for, 22-23
and nonexistent problems, 37
pitfalls in, 27
traps in, 27-28
procrastination
and information search, 78
reasons for, 77-78
types of, 75

quantifiable and unquantifiable factors, 136-138
quick decisions, 9, 10
quick thinking
appearance of, 113-114
developing ability in, 111, 112-114
in noncritical decisions, 117-118
retaining composure, during, 113
under pressure, 110-111

quick thinking *(continued)*
value of, 110-112
vs. snap decisions, 114-115

rationalization, 84-85
recordkeeping, 106
regret, anticipatory, 81
rejection, of decision, 171-172
risk(s)
dealing with, 44-46
and delay, 46
ignoring, 82
and procrastination, 77-78
and selecting alternatives, 157-158
unavoidable, 45
uncertainty and, 136
when not to take, 45-46
risk analysis, 146-148, 149
routine decisions, 3-4
rumors, 124-126

safety issues, 96-98
self-confidence
definition of, 12-13
in making decisions, 13-16
self-improvement, 68-69, 174-175
span-of-control principle, 70
staff meetings, 131-132
statistical analysis, 140-141
strategy, 5-6, 9-10, 16-18
stress
change as, 25
and decision making, 10-12, 55-57, 80
and employee disloyalty, 87-88
and evaluating decisions, 168
external pressure as, 84
intensity of, 56
poor ways of coping with, 11
possible regret as, 80

stress *(continued)*

positive ways of dealing with, 56-57
symptoms of, 10-11
subordinates, *see* employees
supervisor(s)
attitudes toward safety, 97
and controversy, 85-86
explaining decisions to subordinates, 132-133
and gossip, 124-126
effectiveness of, 3
and employee acceptance of decisions, 51
and employee loyalty, 86-87
fallibility of, 8
and meetings with members of staff, 131-132
mobility of, 30
and operations researchers, 146
praise as tool of, 50-52

supervisors *(continued)*

and procrastination, 75-77
responsibility of, 3, 31
and self-evaluation, 2
and time management, 107-110
and unions, 44
supervisor-employee relationships, 47-48, 53, 54-55, 132-133

task forces, *see* group decision making
techniques, decision making, *see* strategy
time management, 107-110
trade-offs, 58

workers, *see* employees
worry, circumstances causing, 81-84